Unstoppable

CHANGING OUR MINDSETS
AND UNLOCKING OUR FUTURE
A devotional journey

CWR

Other titles in this series by Jen Baker:

Untangled

Finding freedom today and hope for tomorrow

Unlimited

Knowing our identity and finding our purpose

Contents

Introduction

I'm so pleased you have chosen to join me in changing your mindsets and creating unstoppable faith – I believe it will literally be life-changing for you!

Of all the books I've written, I am most excited about this one because of the way my life and walk with God has been changed through learning what's in these pages.

Over the next 12 weeks, we will study the mindsets we carry – the negative ones (the lies) that hold us back, and the positive ones (the truth) that can propel us forward – and how they affect our everyday lives, patterns and responses.

In 1 Corinthians 2:16 we read that 'we have the mind of Christ'. What a phenomenal thought! God does not want us to live in confusion regarding His ways, or in fear over His plans. He *wants* us to spiritually discern His character, nature and will, trusting Him further as we know Him deeper.

And one way to deepen our spiritual knowledge is to learn and continually meditate on the truth of His Word until *His truth becomes our belief*. Because what we believe affects every area of our lives.

In the first six weeks of this book, we will explore negative mindsets that keep us from fully embracing the positive truths necessary for an overcoming lifestyle.

Overarching every negative mindset is *fear*. We won't be looking at fear specifically, because as we choose to confront and replace old thinking, we gain greater grounding in God's Word; and hearing the Word brings faith; and by faith we know love; and perfect love casts out all fear.

We will begin by looking at the top three questions I believe everyone asks:

Do you love me?
Do you want me?
Do you need me?

Exploring these questions will get us ready to attack negative mindsets often created as a result of the lies we have believed: loneliness, rejection and anger. During the first six weeks we will establish truth as a foundation in place of the lies we have grown to believe.

Then, in Part 2, we build on these foundations, establishing six positive mindsets to carry us onwards into an overcoming lifestyle.

I pray you will be blessed, set free and, most importantly, that your relationship with the Lord will go to a level of intimacy you previously thought impossible.

Seek Him with all your heart... He promises you *will* find Him.

Much love,

THANK YOU

First and foremost, I thank my Heavenly Father, Jesus Christ and the Holy Spirit for being the best Friends a girl could ever desire. I love You more than any words could ever hope to express.

My parents. You have been my rock throughout it all. For your endless and unfailing love, prayers and support; for believing in me long before I ever believed in myself... thank you. *I love you* doesn't scratch the surface of how I feel about you.

Tammi, Werner, Bobby, Kimi. Though an ocean separates us, you are always in my heart and on my mind. I love how we love one another, despite the fact we could not be more different. Thanks for being friends as well as family.

Penelope, Dorothy and Hobbes. You have my heart.

Lisa. You are a loyal friend, indescribable help, prayer warrior and secret weapon for the kingdom. For everything – *thank you.*

Shari. You are braver than you know. Walk in that bravery. I'll always be cheering you on.

Bri. Your future is amazing; thank you for letting me have a small part in helping it unfold.

Leslie. Your future is rock solid beyond all imagining.

Lynette, Katie, Rebecca, Lucy and the entire CWR family who make me sound so much better than I am, thank you! You have been unceasingly patient, endlessly helpful and always encouraging. I love journeying with you – let's do another sometime soon.

Kerry, Tanja, Judith, Beth, Phil, Gill, Chrissy, Brian, Sylvia. You held up my arms when my strength was gone for so many months... *THANK YOU.*

I dedicate this book to Bev Murrill. An outstanding woman of God who has mentored and taught me more than she will ever know. Bev, your life exemplifies everything this book endeavours to express. Forever and always, thank you.

Part 1

The Lies

NEGATIVE MINDSETS THAT HOLD US BACK

Week 1

'I'm not loved'

'For God so loved the world, that he gave his only Son, that whoever believes in him should not perish but have eternal life.' (John 3:16)

Monday

I'm starting to write this book from the comfort of my friends' lovely country home, tucked away in a beautifully quaint village in the north of England. In addition to fabulous hospitality, they have a nearly four-year-old boy and a four-month-old girl – which, I'm sure you'd agree, creates a beautifully calming environment conducive to writing…

OK, maybe it's not like writing from a seaside villa in Greece (oh… may *that* be prophetic, Lord!), but it's perfect for me at this moment because it's an environment of love. And as I'm traversing a difficult season, being in a place filled with people who love me (though I think the boy is still weighing out his verdict) is life-giving and joy renewing.

Love will do that.

It reassures us that we are okay when others have told us we are not; and it invites us in when life has seemingly shut the door.

And after spending time here, I'm convinced one of the purest forms of love is found in the eyes of a newborn.

Being godmother to baby Beatrice is a true honour and I love her as my own. I treasure the countless times she has fallen asleep in my arms and I adore her toothless smile, which literally lights up her entire little face.

But one of the greatest joys is seeing our 'friend', who appears several times a day. If at any point Bea is a bit grizzly, I carry her over to the large mirror in the sitting room. There we peer into the glass and – like magic – our little friend is always right there to greet us! And it's a real coincidence that her tiny face lights up exactly to the measure of Beatrice's, which only delights her more, and on it goes. It is a beautiful sight to behold and could warm even the coldest of hearts.

She's far too young to understand the theory behind glass and reflection, but she understands the beauty – and joy – of acceptance and love found in a baby's eyes. It is non-judgmental, colourblind, and innocent... the way love should be.

I wonder, at what age does that change? When do we start putting conditions on that love, maybe not for a baby but for our neighbour, friend or spouse? Has our love become conditional on having our expectations met before we allow it to be released?

I'm not waiting for the perfection of a seaside villa to write a book – nor should we wait for someone to be lovable before we love.

We love because He first loved us, full stop.

Father, I pray Your love will be unveiled to me in a new way this week. In the past I have put up walls, hidden and pushed You away out of fear of rejection and shame. I no longer want to live this way. Please show me how to receive Your love in fullness, trusting You to hold my heart tenderly and lovingly. Amen.

Tuesday

Let's begin our journey with prayer, because looking at mindsets – where they began and how they've become what they are – can at times be a painful process. Remember the Lord's promises: He is for us and not against us; He will never leave us nor forsake us and He works all things together for our good.

So, Father, I thank You for being with my sister right now where she is sitting. I ask You, precious Holy Spirit, to comfort, guide, direct and counsel her along this journey. I thank You that all good gifts come from You and that walking in freedom is the best gift we could ever receive! May Your truths be seen in new ways and Your life be received in full measure. I take authority over any spirit of fear in the name of Jesus, and I declare freedom in place of fear. Thank You for helping us renew our minds with the truth. Amen.

One of the most important things you will do over the coming weeks is to begin to notice what you are thinking about. The Bible says that from the overflow of the heart the mouth speaks; so check in on your thoughts – are they positive or negative? I've noticed I can easily be deceived into believing my mindset is positive, but when I listen to my words I hear quite a bit of negativity coming out of my mouth!

As we meditate on the Word, we will:

- be firmly planted
- yield fruit in season
- not wither
- prosper in all things.

Wow! Who else wants to be immovable, fruitful and prosperous?

Sadly, most of us do not grow up knowing these truths and so we meditate on lies from the world, leaving us vulnerable to storms, plagued by doubt and full of fear.

As children, we subconsciously seek validation from those around us and if that validation isn't received, or is perceived as not being given, we can create a negative mindset – opening the door for the enemy to create a belief system based on a lie.

But our tomorrow need not look like our today; His mercies are new every morning and His Spirit is there to help and guide us.

Meditate on Psalm 1, then write how you are feeling about moving forward.

Wednesday

W e all long to be loved. It's human nature and comes from the author of love Himself. God *is* love (1 John 4:8), and we are made in the image of God, therefore love is intricately and intimately a part of who we are in Christ.

As mentioned yesterday, the enemy seeks to destroy us from an early age. Some of you may have painful memories where the word 'love' took on an unholy form. Or maybe the love that should have been free and unconditional came at a cost from a parent, sibling or friend.

This can create a lie early in life that says 'I am unlovable'. And if this lie isn't dealt with, it becomes the soil for seeds of more lies to grow.

Can you think of a relationship or situation you had early in life where you felt love was withheld from you?

....

....

Ask the Holy Spirit to reveal what lie you believed as a result of that relationship or event.

....

....

We view the world through the thoughts we believe, so if someone believes they are unlovable they could, for example, treat any type of disagreement as rejection – even if it wasn't intended that way.

Can you see any patterns in your life that have been developed as a result of believing a lie about love?

John 8:1–11 portrays a beautiful story of true love. Here we see that love does not blame, shame or play games. It is open, honest, vulnerable and without demands. Jesus does not expose or focus on this woman's sin; He declares freedom from condemnation and exhorts her to walk in her newfound freedom as the beautiful daughter of God she was created to be.

Close your eyes. Picture Jesus coming into the room where you are sitting. Let Him sit as close to you as you are comfortable, and then *listen* as He says how much He loves you. Let His words of affirmation wash over you. Don't worry about 'making this up' – God is love and He enjoys reminding us of His love.

Write down what you hear God saying to you. Ask the Holy Spirit for the courage to believe in His love.

Thursday

A uthor Michael Hyatt says, 'God is the one Person who is wholly other-centered. He made us in his image and delights in us. He stubbornly loves us even when we are unlovable. If that's not validation, I don't know what is.'[1]

As we've looked this week at the desire for love and the lies we may have believed, let us now focus on how we are *truly* seen by heaven.

Read the following scriptures a few times slowly, letting the validation of them settle over you:

'Open up before God, keep nothing back; he'll do whatever needs to be done: He'll validate your life in the clear light of day and stamp you with approval at high noon.'
(Psa. 37:5–6, *The Message*)

'How blessed is God! And what a blessing he is! He's the Father of our Master, Jesus Christ, and takes us to the high places of blessing in him. Long before he laid down earth's foundations, he had us in mind, had settled on us as the focus of his love, to be made whole and holy by his love. Long, long ago he decided to adopt us into his family through Jesus Christ. (What pleasure he took in planning this!) He wanted us to enter into the celebration of his lavish gift-giving by the hand of his beloved Son.' (Eph. 1:3–6, *The Message*)

Notice that there is NO requirement for change before these scriptures are true in your life; they are true right now!

Below, write what God wants to do in your life according to these scriptures and how that makes you feel.

....

....

....

I want to close today by dwelling on God's validation of you. Take a few deep breaths and repeat the following statements *out loud*:

I am deeply loved by God – right now.

I am fully accepted by God – right now.

I have purpose in this world as I am – right now.

I am more than an overcomer in Christ.

I am blessed and highly favoured.

I am blessed to bless others.

I can do all things through Christ who strengthens me.

It's understandable if you find them difficult to say. The more you speak truth, the faster the lies will be broken. Imagine each sentence like a new seed planted in your heart – it will take time for the seed to grow, but it *will* grow eventually.

Friday

It's impossible in one week to deal fully with the issues of identity and validation. But what this devotional seeks to do is open the door to truths that you can then build into your belief system, cement into your spirit and use to redirect your thought life.

By doing this, new habits will be formed and a new you *will* emerge.

The Bible says not to grow weary in doing good. Every choice you make to think a new thought will reap a harvest of blessing if you keep watering it with your faith and don't give in to the lies of the enemy.

Read John 15:9–17 and write out below the verse(s) that jump out at you.

....

....

....

....

....

....

The Message Bible translates verse 9 as: 'I've loved you the way my Father has loved me. Make yourselves at home in my love.'

What would it look like for you to make yourself at home in God's love?

....

....

....

....

....

....

God, thank You for loving me as I am right now. Even if I never changed, You would still love and accept me. I am choosing today to abide in You and ask that You teach me the Father's love in a new way over the next 11 weeks. Amen.

Week 2

'I'm not important'

'Fear not, for I have redeemed you;

I have called you by name, you are mine.'

(Isa. 43:1)

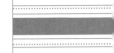

Monday

S heep are bizarre creatures.

To me, they are not particularly attractive, they are dirty, smelly and – let's be honest – not very intelligent. They eat, poop, sleep, stare, repeat.

Yet whenever I have walked the stunning country lanes of England, whether in North Yorkshire or South Devon, I have noticed that as I pass by, the sheep look at me as if I'm interrupting their very important schedule.

The universal stare of, 'Who are you and why are you bothering me?' is evident from the moors to the dales. It is like they have an important day ahead and my presence is threatening to seriously cramp their schedule of eating… and the rest of it.

What is considered important and urgent to one, is simply passing time to another.

Society tells us that acquiring wealth, being known by man and having a pleasing appearance opens doors to acceptance and promotion. And in the world, this is true. If you want to step into the 'inner circle' of any particular organisation or sphere, then developing wealth, status and beauty will most definitely help.

But while we are in the world, we are not of it.

We are sheep, and our Shepherd does things differently.

To Him, importance is not in what one shows but in how one lives. Grass carries a high value for sheep because they were created to eat – and enjoy – it, otherwise their lives would be a complete misery (not to mention short). They are fulfilling their purpose by focusing on the task at hand, which if not done could lead to malnourished bodies, poor wool, unhappy shepherds and a woefully lacking number of socks and jumpers.

On the other hand, if birds were told to sit in a field all day and munch on the meadow, they would hit full-blown depression within 24 hours knowing their wings had, metaphorically, been clipped. They need to soar in order to fulfil purpose.

Both lifestyles are vital to survival, and purpose, yet in completely different ways.

Therefore eating grass is not passing time: it is fulfilling purpose, and in the eyes of the kingdom this is important. Remember Joseph in the prison, Gideon in the wine press, Lazarus in the tomb and Jesus in the desert? The definition of important is on a much different scale in heaven than on earth; what looks like minimal effort to a striving world might be a season of hiddenness necessary to fuel your next breakthrough, from which you will soar to new heights.

There is a big lesson to be learnt from the sheep: if the shepherd has led you to this place, trust Him.

Father, thank You for accepting me as I am right now, in whatever state you find me. Though I might seem 'smelly and unattractive' at times, Your love never ceases and Your arms are always open. Amen.

Tuesday

If last week's question asks 'Do you love me?', then this week we explore 'Do you want me?' We move from knowing we are validated in heaven to wondering if we are accepted on earth.

In the software industry, *validation* and *verification* serve two completely different purposes. Validation is to ensure that the product meets the customer's satisfaction and will be accepted, while verification is to ensure the product is built according to design specification.

In a world that is 'me-focused', it is easy to confuse these two words and think we can use them interchangeably. In other words, we may think, 'If people accept my "design" then I must be designed correctly'.

Just as this wouldn't be the case in the natural world, it should not be the case in the spiritual world. If I only feel important because you have told me that I am, then my identity will be forever tied to your approval.

But if I believe my design matches the specifications of heaven, made in His image, validated by His love and verified by His creation, then although your satisfaction with the 'product' is important to me, it is not vital to my wellbeing.

You've probably heard this phrase: There's nothing you can do to make Him love you more, and there's nothing you can do to make Him love you less. And it's true – God is love. It is not dependent on what you do or how you behave: He loves you because that is His nature and it's impossible for Him not to love a creation made in His own image.

Can you think of anything you are doing or believing right now that, if you are honest, is propelled by the hope that it will increase God's love for you?

....

....

....

In what ways has God verified and validated you? (Gen. 1:26–28; Col. 3:10; Eph. 4:24 will help you get started.)

....

....

....

....

Wednesday

We are going to look at a familiar, and possibly confusing, story in Mark's Gospel today. Read Mark 7:24–30 before you continue.

In this passage, it appears Jesus is speaking harshly to a woman simply because of her 'design' – the fact that she was Greek and not Jewish. There are several things to note, but today we'll just focus on two points of interest.

The word 'dogs' in this passage means 'little dogs', as in the kind that might be a pet in someone's home, not the dirty dogs out on the streets.[2] One commentary notes that it could be similar to saying someone 'is tenacious like a bulldog' – actually a term of endearment and not literally calling them an animal.[3]

But also notice how Jesus uses the word 'first', which this precious woman picks up on. Jesus is prophetically speaking about the Jews receiving salvation first, and then the Gentiles.

Her faith is unmistakable. And Jesus always notices faith!

A woman who looked unimportant to Jesus' disciples and the Jewish community was actually a prophetic symbol of future salvation to nations beyond Israel. Her 'unimportant' presence could not have been more important!

Regardless of how others have seen – or failed to see – you, God sees you.

What would you like Him to see in you that others may not fully see?

....

....

....

....

....

What part of being made in His image blesses you and ministers to you the most?

....

....

....

....

....

Thursday

O n Monday we said, 'importance is not in what one shows but in how one lives'.

In a social media world, we can easily succumb to the pressure of comparing ourselves with those around us.

Steven Furtick says, 'The reason we struggle with insecurity is because we compare our behind-the-scenes with everyone else's highlight reel.'[4]

Have you ever struggled with that? Feeling like you aren't 'measuring up' when you see or hear about the lives of other people, what they have, or what they are doing at a certain stage in their lives?

How much time are you spending on social media right now, and are you at peace with that?

In January, I decided to do a three-week social media fast, and it was one of the best decisions I've ever made. I saw a remarkable difference in how I felt about my life after a few weeks of not comparing it with everyone else's!

I encourage you to consider doing your own 'fast' of social media. Write down what you could do in that time instead of spending it scrolling through 'other people's highlights'.

....
....
....
....

If you decide to start, write here when you are going to begin and end.

....
....
....

What, if anything, makes you most apprehensive about doing this?

....
....
....

Let's spend some extra time today in prayer. I encourage you to find some quiet worship music to play in the background and then set a timer for 5–10 minutes. Take that time *only* thanking God and worshipping Him.

Friday

O ne of my favourite Bible stories is found in John 4 where Jesus is speaking to the Samaritan woman. Some believe she was an outcast due to her life choices; others think she suffered a different form of tragedy with at least a few of her husbands dying natural deaths. Whatever the reason, she was a woman who had been married five times, and at the time Jesus met her was not married to the man she lived with.

In our day her life might raise some eyebrows, but in that day it shouted a warning: *Stay away from this one!*

We have all done things in our past that we aren't proud of and perhaps wished we could reverse or remove. But the reality is that Jesus welcomes us with open arms, regardless of the spiritual or earthly baggage we may carry.

This week as I've been writing, I have sensed that there are some women who need to receive forgiveness from the Lord, and need also to forgive themselves for the choices they have made.

If this doesn't resonate with you then I encourage you to spend the rest of today reading the Samaritan story again, and asking Holy Spirit to highlight a specific scripture to meditate on, then write it down.

. . . .

. . . .

. . . .

If this does resonate with you then I ask that you still yourself before the Lord, look over the scriptures this past week, that have talked about your acceptance in Christ, and when ready, pray the following prayer with me.

Dear Lord, I come to You in repentance today for...

. . . .

. . . .

. . . .

I am truly sorry for what I have done and how I have acted, and I ask that You forgive me for this. Thank You that Your Word says if we confess our sins, You are faithful to forgive them and cleanse us from all unrighteousness (1 John 1:9). I choose now to receive Your forgiveness. I am forgiven, and free from the guilt of this event. I receive Your love and peace right now and I choose to walk free. Amen.

(Then continue with this second prayer...)

I also choose to forgive myself for the things I have done or said that have caused hurt in the lives of others. I will no longer hold myself hostage to regret – instead, in Your name, I break that stronghold over my life and rebuke the lie that says I am not important. I believe the Word of God that says I am the righteousness of God in Christ Jesus (2 Cor. 5:21), and that I have victory and have overcome the world by my faith (1 John 5:4). I choose now to live as a redeemed daughter of the Most High God, loved, forgiven and set free! Amen.

Week 3

'I'm not successful'

'And the King will answer them, "Truly, I say to you, as you did it to one of the least of these my brothers, you did it to me."' (Matt. 25:40)

Monday

The older I get, the more my attention span resembles that of a four-year-old.

Though I'm inclined to blame it on society rather than the number of years I've been alive, I have to wonder if there is a link? They say we become more childlike as we age, reverting to loving simplicity, sleeping in irregular patterns, enjoying blander food and… yeah, the memory thing. I have new respect/understanding for my mother and her love of those little yellow sticky notes… you know the ones I mean!

How is it that I can be deep in the presence of God during my daily morning devotions, and yet within seconds I find that I've updated my Waitrose card, caught up on the news, and now find myself scrolling through random status updates on Facebook?

Fifteen or so years ago, we had to intentionally *choose* distraction – we'd have to sit down to watch television, or physically go to where the phone is plugged in and make a phone-call.

In today's world we have to intentionally *avoid* distraction because we are surrounded by distracting temptations at every turn – computers, smart phones and social media – which, if allowed, are with us 24/7.

At the core of most distraction is the Fear Of Missing Out – FOMO.

What if I miss an important announcement on social media, or the latest 'must watch' series on Netflix, or worse… the latest updates on Brexit?!

We fear not knowing something we 'need' to know and not seeing something that, for those few minutes, might be worth watching. Which makes me wonder if our view of success is often based on the same fear – missing out.

Our lives 'must' appear to be moving forward, our income increasing, our faith strengthening and our family being happier – otherwise we are just not succeeding in life. There's nothing overtly wrong with any of those goals: they are worthy ambitions, but are they the only measuring sticks for success?

Jesus told the rich young ruler to 'sell all… and come, follow me' (Mark 10:17–31), which he was unable to do: success in heaven did not outweigh the success he wanted on earth. True success has never come easy, and 'the road less travelled' is such for a reason.

Following the crowd of the world doesn't require intentionality; forging heaven on earth, however, requires immutable intentionality. For if we are not intentionally seeking Christ in all that we do (Prov. 3:6; Matt. 6:33; Deut. 4:29), the current of the world will pull us off course.

Let's not allow the apparent urgency of today to distract us from the absolute priority of eternal things.

Are you comfortable with the level of time you are giving to social media/television/newspaper? If not, what would you like to change?

....

....

....

....

Tuesday

The negative mindset we are looking to break this week is around the question, 'Do you need me?'

Not only do we long for validation and approval in our lives, we want purpose. And if the enemy can convince us we have none, or that we've missed it or outlived it, then it opens the door for other negative thoughts and feelings (lies) to set up camp and put down roots. So I say let's go after that and *kick them out* because they are severely trespassing on God's property!

Look up the following scriptures and summarise them in your own words: Jeremiah 29:11; Ephesians 2:10; 2 Timothy 1:9.

....

....

....

....

You have been created for a purpose, and I firmly believe that if a person is still breathing, which I assume you are, then that person has purpose this side of heaven. (My book *Unlimited* goes into much more detail throughout its 12-week journey looking at this topic.)

As mentioned earlier, in order to change a mindset, we must get to the root of the lie feeding that mindset. The Holy Spirit is our amazing guide on this journey of life and is here to help you know the mind of the Father and the truth of the Word.

Take a few minutes right now to ask Him what your purpose is in this season of your life. Then write down what you hear.

....

....

....

How have you seen your purpose change over the years that you have been a Christian?

....

....

....

As we grow in faith, God expands our territory (Isa. 54:1–3). So how are you intentionally growing your faith right now? What are you believing for that is beyond your own ability to produce? (If you can't think of something, pray for a brand new God-sized dream!)

....

....

....

Wednesday

Y ou are not your past.

Let me say that again. You are *not* your past.

Whatever has happened up to now does not define who you are becoming. There may be a few darkened brush strokes on your life's canvas, but they are not the full picture. Any good painting will have some darker nuances of colour, however subtle which, when laid against the light, create the whole. Removing some of the darker colours only lessens the intensity of the bright and hampers the overall image.

If I have learned anything in this faith-walk, it is that what looks like a 'dark spot' on my painting of life is often the beginning of the most beautiful strokes of my journey's picture – and I tamper with the artist at great cost to the overall beauty of what He is creating. 'Hands off!' is a good phrase to remember!

Let God do what He wants to do, regardless of how you've arrived at this particular season of life.

Think back on your journey and write down some beautiful gifts that have arisen unexpectedly out of difficult circumstances.

....

....

....

What are your biggest barriers to fully trusting the Lord with this season?

....

....

....

Now write out what you would define as a 'success' for this particular season of your life. Allow yourself to envision it, dream it, picture it and then journal it.

....

....

....

Thursday

You have been chosen. For a purpose. Which extends beyond you.

'For he chose us in him before the creation of the world to be holy and blameless in his sight.' (Eph. 1:4, NIVUK)

'Your eyes saw my unformed body; all the days ordained for me were written in your book before one of them came to be.' (Psa. 139:16, NIVUK)

'For we are his workmanship, created in Christ Jesus for good works, which God prepared beforehand, that we should walk in them.' (Eph. 2:10)

'For I know the plans I have for you, declares the LORD, plans for welfare and not for evil, to give you a future and a hope. Then you will call upon me and come and pray to me, and I will hear you. You will seek me and find me, when you seek me with all your heart.' (Jer. 29:11–13)

'But you will receive power when the Holy Spirit has come upon you, and you will be my witnesses in Jerusalem and in all Judea and Samaria, and to the end of the earth.' (Acts 1:8)

Read the above verses out loud, and insert *your name* wherever it says 'we' or 'you'. Make it personal and read them over a few times. Even if you've heard them a hundred times, pretend you haven't, and allow the truth to wash over you as if it was the first reading.

You have been chosen.

For a purpose.

Which extends beyond you.

Now say out loud: *I have been chosen, for a purpose, which extends beyond me.*

What is your 'beyond me'? What dreams do you have that will impact (or are already impacting) someone who can never give back to you or who may never know the investment you have made into their life? Write about it here and then pray.

....

....

....

....

....

Father, today we again freely choose to serve You and Your purposes for us. We pray in agreement with 1 Chronicles 4:10, which asks You to bless us, enlarge our territory, put Your hand on us, and keep us from harm that we might not cause pain. May this ring true in our own lives today and may You be honoured by the love we show to those around us. Amen.

Friday

Quoting Scripture is one thing, but believing it is another. Believing is what opens the door to receiving our breakthrough. It is all about revelation, not recitation.

And revelation comes when we let our spirit take hold of the truth, not just our mind.

Walking in revelation is also what allows our mindsets to remain changed for the better and for the long-term, not just temporarily adjusted. If I quote scriptures by recitation that is good, but there is no guarantee that they will move from my head to my heart. But if I have a heart revelation of the truth, then no amount of argument will ever take that away – my spirit has taken hold of it.

For example, I became a Christian at the age of 19 but I didn't really have a revelation of that decision until a few weeks after the fact. It was that revelation of the truth that then changed my behaviour, not the other way around.

In John 6:69, Peter says, 'and we have believed, and have come to know, that you are the Holy One of God.' Belief came first – then *knowing* followed.

Teaching on the power of belief would be another book entirely, but let's scratch the surface here by asking yourself: Do I *really* believe what the scriptures I've read this week say about me?

If you cannot honestly answer 'yes', that's OK. The more you read them, meditate on them (that is important), and ask the Holy Spirit to reveal the truth of them to you, the more you will begin moving towards revelation. Receive them by faith. Not only with your head, but with heart-faith. And faith comes from hearing through the Word of Christ (Rom. 10:17), so feed your spirit with these truths every day until they become more real to you than the negativity you have been believing.

It may be worth pausing your time in this book and taking another full week to review the scriptures you have read these past few weeks. Repeat them regularly, ideally out loud, inserting your name and believing they are yours. As you do this, I pray that you will slowly begin to feel a shift in your belief system, in your thoughts, and eventually in your behaviours.

Lord, I pray You will be my sister's strength, guide, cheerleader, companion and reminder of truth. if at any point she moves into negative thinking, please convict her of her righteousness in You and remind her of who she is in Christ, according to these scriptures. Amen.

Week 4

'I'm alone'

'for He [God] Himself has said, I will not in
any way fail you *nor* give you up *nor* leave
you without support. [I will] not, [I will] not,
[I will] not in any degree leave you helpless
nor forsake *nor* let [you] down (relax My
hold on you)! [Assuredly not!]'
(Heb. 13:5, AMPC)

Monday

'In memory of Harry and Edna Witheford.'

These words, etched on a plaque, grace one simple, wooden bench off the side of a road overlooking the fields of North Yorkshire. Surrounded by rolling hills, horses, sheep and a gentle breeze, one could imagine Harry and Edna sipping a cup of tea while passing the days together on this corner.

Sitting on 'their' bench, I imagined what their lives might have been like and how many years they were together. Were they happy years? Did they get used to the stunning view that God had given them to oversee? Who is the new keeper of the corner, so to speak, or does it remain dedicated to their memory only?

Though we don't know the answers to those questions, I like to imagine them madly in love until death did them part.

Love, by definition, needs companionship and an object for its affection. This was the purpose behind creation – the one who *is* love created us as an outlet to *express* love.

Though the Trinity shared perfect love among themselves, they knew their love could extend vastly further. As we saw last week, before we were formed in our mother's womb He knew us (Jer. 1:5; Psa. 139:16) and chose us for an intended purpose.

And that purpose has never been isolation.

As Harry had Edna, so the Godhead has each of us.

Imagine a bench somewhere that simply says, 'In celebration of the Father, Son, Holy Spirit and [insert your name here]'. And that is where you all sit together enjoying the view of life, noticing nuances that weren't there the day before and breathing in the changing winds of time with each new season. Laughing together, sometimes crying together, being together side by side for all of eternity.

As we grow comfortable on that bench we are freed to sit on benches with others. We gain confidence to walk up the road a bit and etch our name side by side with others on this same journey, creating benches of memories that we can revisit anytime we like. There is no competition on the number of benches, as the fields of possibility are endless and the views ever-changing with each new friendship.

It's amazing what a bench will tell you.

What will yours say?

. . . .

. . . .

. . . .

. . . .

PS – I've just searched for Harry's name on the internet to see what I could find out about him. It turns out he was the 17th person to volunteer for the Indian Army at the outbreak of the Second World War, was captured by the Japanese, survived torturous conditions, then finally returned home to his beloved Edna, with whom he shared 62 wonderful married years.

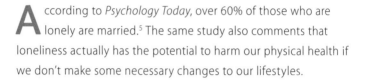

Tuesday

According to *Psychology Today*, over 60% of those who are lonely are married.[5] The same study also comments that loneliness actually has the potential to harm our physical health if we don't make some necessary changes to our lifestyles.

I am sure all of you reading this right now have felt, or are feeling, lonely in your life. It is nothing to be embarrassed about and is, in fact, extremely common. The older we become as women, the more it can sneak up on us if we aren't careful, especially with the changing seasons of kids leaving the house, possible career changes, changes in our marital status, moving cities or retiring. Suddenly our social circle begins to change and we wonder where we belong, and to whom?

I've been single all my life and about five years ago, when I was 42, someone asked me if I was lonely. I responded honestly, 'No, I'm not lonely… I'm alone.' There is a difference. I have spent over twenty years living alone, not by choice I might add (!), and yes there are times I feel twinges of loneliness. But I have learned to see it as living alone, not being lonely.

Part of overcoming this in my own life was intentionally choosing my thoughts on the situation. I intentionally chose to be *thankful* for the many things I could do as a single person living alone, not the least for hanging out with Ben and Jerry for dinner whenever I wanted! (Ben and Jerry's is *the* most amazing ice cream, for those who may be uninitiated.)

For whatever reason, you may be feeling lonely – but I gently encourage you to think of some things you can be thankful about, even in this loneliness.

....

....

....

....

....

....

....

....

The Bible says to 'rejoice in the Lord always' (Phil. 4:4) and 'give thanks in all circumstances' (1 Thess. 5:18), so let's close today with some thanksgiving!

Again I'd like you to set the timer and spend *at least* five minutes thanking the Lord. Don't ask for anything – *thank* Him. If necessary, thank Him for the same things over and over, thank Him for every possible thing you can think of, and then… thank Him again. He is worthy of all our praise!

Wednesday

C hanging mindsets means intentionally choosing new thoughts.

So let's focus on that a bit more today...

Write out Philippians 4:8 below.

. . . .

. . . .

. . . .

This is how it's written in *The Message*:

> 'Summing it all up, friends, I'd say you'll do best by filling
> your minds and meditating on things true, noble, reputable,
> authentic, compelling, gracious—the best, not the worst; the
> beautiful, not the ugly; things to praise, not things to curse.'

I love how this says 'filling your minds' and 'meditating', as that is the key to breakthrough. I'm sure you've heard the saying, 'What we think, we will say; and what we say, we will eventually do'. The power of our mind and our words cannot be underestimated; it is one of our greatest weapons against the lies of the enemy.

I asked you earlier to begin to take notice of what you are thinking about. Have you done that? What have you discovered? (If you haven't consciously done this yet, then I would encourage you to do so in order to get the most out of the devotional and to see breakthrough in your thought life.)

....

....

....

I looked up Philippians 4:8 in 25 different versions of the Bible and they *all* started the list with the word TRUE. Meditating on the truth is *very* important to God!

What is occupying most of your thought life at the moment? Thinking about that, are your thoughts dwelling on things you *know* to be absolutely true (according to the Word of God)?

....

....

....

....

....

....

Thursday

Yesterday we looked at Philippians 4:8 and the importance of intentionally meditating on the truth.

One thing we must always remember is that the Word of God is our absolute truth and it overrides 'fact' every single time. If the Word promises me one thing and my circumstances are showing me another, there is no question in my mind: the Word is what I believe.

If this is not our solid foundation then we are standing on shifting sand, as our feelings and circumstances will always be swaying between positive and negative, due to the world we live in and the spiritual battles we face.

So, is there anything in your life right now that is making it difficult for you to trust the Word?

. . . .

. . . .

. . . .

Do you believe God is good? (Read the following scriptures if there is any doubt: Psa. 31:19–20; 34:8; 84:11; 100:5; 135:3; 145; Lam. 3:25; Matt. 7:11; Rom. 8:28; James 1:17.)

Do you believe He is *for* you (Rom. 8:31)?

Write out your own prayer to God thanking Him for His goodness in your life. If you are struggling to see Him as good at the moment, express this honestly to Him, and then ask for His help to show you His goodness in your life.

....

....

....

....

....

....

....

....

Finally, take a few minutes to sit in stillness and quiet. Ask Him to reveal the beauty of His love to you in a new way.

Friday

As children of God, it is impossible for us to ever be alone.

We always have our three companions – Father, Son and Holy Spirit – on the journey with us. Getting to know each of them is vitally important to knowing all of them, as they are one, yet separate. This is a truth too complex to explore in this book, but true and beautiful nonetheless!

As you think about the different roles they play in your life, which one of the Godhead are you most comfortable with and why?

Now imagine that one (Father, Son or Holy Spirit) sitting with you in your home (or wherever you are reading this), enjoying the time together. Then pray the following prayer with me:

Dear Lord, thank You for being with me right now. And I thank You Jesus for the blood You shed for my salvation. I ask right now for Your peace to be in this place, covering me with Your protection and shielding me from harm. My ears are open to hear Your voice only, and I thank You in advance for speaking to me. Amen.

Now ask Him what He thinks of you. (He will only speak positively, so if you hear anything negative, you can say out loud that you do not accept lies and once again ask the Lord to speak to you.) Write below what He says and receive this truth into your spirit.

....

....

....

....

....

Meditating on God's love for us and the truth of His Word will help free us from loneliness. I am not guaranteeing everything to be better within a day or a week, but as you intentionally let these verses and this exercise become routine for you, then you will begin to build a stronger relationship with the Lord, and know a peace you may have previously been missing.

We began the week thinking of Harry and Edna sitting on their bench together. Imagine you are sitting there now with the Lord; what would you chat about?

....

....

....

....

....

Week 5

'I'm rejected'

'even as he chose us in him before the foundation of the world, that we should be holy and blameless before him. In love he predestined us for adoption to himself as sons through Jesus Christ, according to the purpose of his will' (Eph. 1:4–5)

Monday

Have you ever felt you were a bystander in your own life story?

I often feel like life is running past me, and instead of throwing myself into the current play on the field, I'm getting run over as I stand immobile and confused just trying to understand what's happening.

Do I hear an 'Amen'?!

Being a single adult, this feeling may be more prevalent for me, but I tend to think we all struggle at times with feeling left out of the game called Life.

Years ago, my best friend and I dreamed of raising our kids as friends and arranging playdates at each other's homes. Soon she had one, and then another, and it didn't take long to realise that dream would never come to pass – as I seemingly couldn't even move my backside off the bench and onto the field of relationships and family.

I tried to enjoy the single life, yet deep inside I ached for the family life. Ironically, as I was aching for marriage and children, she, with little sleep and now three precious little boys, was envious of my put-together look and carefree lifestyle.

As it turned out, I moved overseas to England where the dream of us raising children together died once and for all. In England, I developed new friendships, and those friends soon had their own children, and the dream of raising kids together repeated itself, several times over.

At the age of 47, and still yet to be married, I no longer have those conversations with friends.

And yes, it is painful.

Often I've felt like a homeless child out in the cold on Christmas morning, peering through the window of a perfect family enjoying their perfect Christmas Day by the perfectly warm fireplace, wondering what it would be like to know that reality; always on the outside looking in.

Thankfully I've learned that perfection doesn't exist.

We are all simultaneously participating in life *and* watching it pass us by. I don't believe any woman, regardless of personal circumstances, has gone her entire life without ever wondering what she was doing, was this all worth it and is this the life she was meant to live?

The apostle Paul said that he learned to be content in all circumstances; in other words, there were moments when he wasn't content and he had a choice to make. Possibly he was watching when he wanted to participate, or vice versa. Either way, he needed to choose a new mindset and intentionally walk out what he believed, learning contentment through the process.

My friend and I never shared play dates with our children; in fact, due to moving overseas, I have sadly missed the majority of her kids' growing-up years.

Yet we have both participated in each other's stories, sometimes scoring touchdowns and other times wincing from injury.

Perhaps standing by, yet never a bystander.

Father, I want to know Your acceptance on a deeper level this week. Thank You that the door to Your love is always open. Amen.

Tuesday

Rejection – be it a reality or simply a perception in our lives – can become an ingrained mindset that hinders us from stepping into all that God has planned for us.

Seeds of rejection are often planted at a very young age by a family member or life experience, which tells us that we are not wanted or accepted. We can even be affected in the womb if our birth mother did not fully rejoice in our existence.

While this book is not intended to go deep into healing those hurts (I strongly encourage you to seek Christian help if you find any of these chapters touch a deep wound in your life), it is helpful to identify where or when the lie of rejection first came into our belief system.

Ask the Holy Spirit to gently remind you where rejection may have been planted in your heart.

Let Jesus sit with you again (we're going to get pretty good at this!) as close to you as you are comfortable, and when you are ready write out Psalm 27:10 in your own words.

How do you feel knowing that He accepts you, regardless of how others may treat you?

....

....

....

Often the enemy brings confusion by tempting us to follow our feelings and not the truth of the Word. You may not *feel* like the Lord accepts you right now, but all throughout the Bible we see that 'saving and restoring' are His specialties.

By faith, write out a prayer of thanksgiving to Him for loving and accepting you; tell Him what you are most thankful for about Psalm 27:10. Thank Him that He knows the sting of rejection, and that because of His great love for you, He chose to be rejected so that you might be accepted.

....

....

....

....

....

Lord, thank You for never leaving me and never forsaking me; for watching over me when I am afraid, weeping with me when I weep and rejoicing when I rejoice. I receive your acceptance of me and ask that even this week You will show me Your love in a new way. Amen.

Wednesday

Renewing our minds takes effort and intentionality. I am purposefully repeating myself on that point as it is key to your breakthrough and seeing your mindset shift! It is the Word that brings freedom and life, and the more we think on the Word and see it as the final authority in our lives, the quicker we will begin to think differently and see a shift in our circumstances. But we *must* be diligent to study it, believe it and speak it from our mouths repeatedly.

So with that, let's look at more scriptures that tell us how we are seen and loved in heaven.

Write out Romans 8:31 below.

. . . .

. . . .

. . . .

There is absolutely *nothing* more powerful than God. No sin, sickness, disease, challenge, rejection, addiction, short-coming, memory or unbelief is more powerful than God's ability to bring healing and breakthrough.

The Bible also says God is love (1 John 4:8), so we can say with total certainty that nothing is more powerful than the love of God towards your life.

He LOVES you. Let that sink in right now.

NOTHING can separate you from the deep love He holds in His heart for you.

The Message writes Romans 8:38–39 this way:

> 'I'm absolutely convinced that nothing—nothing living or dead, angelic or demonic, today or tomorrow, high or low, thinkable or unthinkable—absolutely *nothing* can get between us and God's love because of the way that Jesus our Master has embraced us.'

So let's take a minute to be honest and write here what things in your life right now feel more powerful than Him.

....

....

....

Then I want you to write in capital letters the following statement: THESE THINGS FEEL POWERFUL, BUT *THEY ARE NOT* MORE POWERFUL THAN GOD'S POWER IN MY LIFE.

....

....

....

Finally, take a few minutes to thank Him for the power of His love and His promise to never leave you.

Thursday

The Amplified Bible says in Romans 8:1:

> 'Therefore there is now no condemnation [no guilty verdict, no punishment] for those who are in Christ Jesus [who believe in Him as personal Lord and Saviour]'.

So please stop condemning yourself.

Each time we criticise, condemn or berate ourselves, it is like hooking a chain to our ankle and chaining ourselves to a weight we must now drag along with us throughout our everyday lives. We would never do that in the natural – so why do that in the spiritual?

Jesus Christ died to take all our sin, shame and punishment in order to give us a life of freedom, joy, peace, blessing and favour, not to mention an eternity in heaven. What an exchange!

Yet I can easily short-circuit those blessings by believing lies about myself that He does not believe, thereby never receiving the fullness of all He died to give me.

We break the power of condemnation through the power of belief.

Write out a declaration of belief here, proclaiming that you will believe the Word above your feelings and circumstances from this day forward. Draw a metaphorical line in the sand today!

....

....

....

....

Joyce Meyer says, 'Self-improvement does not come through self-effort; it comes from dependence upon God – from faith in Him.'[6]

Will you trust that He is bigger than your pain? Read the following scriptures and summarise the truth of them below: Hebrews 7:25; John 10:10; Romans 12:2.

....

....

....

....

....

....

....

Friday

I believe the only way we will overcome rejection is by faith.

Knowing we are saved, accepted and loved by our Father in heaven, we must choose by faith to believe those truths over any other word or action spoken or done against us here on earth.

We will *never* be fully accepted here because this is not our home (Heb. 13:14). I'm sure you've heard the phrase 'hurting people hurt people'. They do and they always will.

Can we say with the apostle Paul, 'For am I now seeking the approval of man, or of God? Or am I trying to please man? If I were still trying to please man, I would not be a servant of Christ.' (Gal. 1:10)?

Write out some practical steps you can take to make sure you are finding your acceptance in God and not in other people.

....

....

....

....

Whose voice do you need to begin drowning out with the truth of the Word of God?

....

....

....

You may have people in your life that you need to (kindly) begin spending less time with, if they are speaking negative and hurtful words to you, and not seeing you as Christ sees you. I realise there may be people you cannot completely separate from (family members or a spouse), and in this case I encourage you to speak to a spiritual authority in your life for some advice.

But remember, your thoughts are *your* thoughts – only you can choose what you will think on; nobody does that for you. And as you begin thinking on things that are true and seeing yourself *fully* accepted by the Lord, then your behaviour will begin to imitate one who is confident in Christ, not dependent on man.

Father, I pray for my sister to have the courage necessary to make the changes required. I pray she gets the revelation of who she is in Christ and how much she is loved by heaven. Rejoice over her today with Your favour and blessings, and show her the next steps necessary to a life of freedom. Amen.

Week 6

'I'm angry'

'Gracious words are like a honeycomb, sweetness to the soul and health to the body.' (Prov. 16:24)

Monday

Confession: I'm afraid of cows.

I don't mean they make me a little uneasy; I mean my heart rate increases, breathing becomes shallow, palms get sweaty and my mind goes into overdrive. Even if I see a small herd at a distance, one lapsed moment into imagination and suddenly they all look like bovine bullies with a licence to kill, and I imagine if not for the wire fence I'd soon be a human carpet beneath their cloven claws. (OK, hooves.)

No, I didn't have a childhood accident where I was hit by a Hereford or stomped on by a steer; I just see something in their eyes that moves beyond disconcerting to something more... demonic.

(Let's be honest, an animal that regurgitates his breakfast to eat a mid-day snack must have issues.)

Recently, I was walking through a field with a friend and her kids when I spotted them – standing a fair distance away – staring. All I could think of was the children. I began looking for the nearest exit, trying to decide which child to grab first and bemoaning the blasted wellies I was wearing in place of trainers. In ten seconds flat I went from relaxed to near panic attack.

Don't judge me – I am sure you've had your irrational moments too, ladies!

How many times have we created false scenarios in our minds that created something less than total peace in our hearts?

We are *certain* that friend was talking about us; the husband forgot on purpose; the mother-in-law disapproves; or the employer isn't happy. And the more we dwell on what *hasn't* yet been proven true, the more intense our anxiety or anger becomes.

Anger is born in our thoughts, but matures in our imagination and creates a permanent home deep down in our heart. Once settled there, we have little chance of mounting a rescue mission and restoring peace unless it's led by the grace of God.

In reality the cows didn't attack, or even move an inch, throughout our entire journey across the top of their field. I suppose the effort to attack wasn't worth it for something that wasn't actually a threat.

Which leads me to wonder, is the source of my anger a genuine threat in my life today, or has truth been overridden by imagination?

Maybe I need to take a lesson from the cows and simply stand my ground, watch the storm pass and, as a result, keep my peace?

Father, as we move into this week looking at the mindset of anger, I ask that You would help me shift the spotlight from others and put it on my own heart. Give me grace to see what You want me to see and do what You ask me to do, knowing Your motive is always my freedom and that victory is already mine through You. Amen.

Tuesday

The Bible says it is OK to feel angry, but not to let the sun go down on your anger (Eph. 4:26).

Anger in itself is not always wrong, but allowing it to stay is not only unbiblical – it is unwise.

Interestingly enough the very next verse says to 'give no opportunity to the devil' (Eph. 4:27). Because when we allow anger to remain, even for a short period of time, we open the door to the enemy and invite him into our atmosphere.

Of course, some of you have very legitimate reasons for being angry with someone or at a situation. When you have suffered great injustice or abuse it seems only 'fair' to remain angry at that person. I was raped at the age of six, have endured betrayal from good Christians on more than one occasion and have been emotionally abused by different men and women over the years. By the world's standards, I have every right to carry anger in my heart.

And yet right now, I can honestly say that, to my knowledge, I do not hold a single grudge or anger toward anyone in my life today.

But, believe me when I say, this has come at a cost, and through many intentional choices such as receiving help and support from others – *all* of which were well worth making.

Before we go further this week, let the Holy Spirit bring to mind any anger you are holding in your heart against someone or as a response to something someone has said or done. As in previous weeks, don't *try* too hard to think of something, but if something does come to mind, write it below.

....

....

....

....

....

We will go into more detail this week, but let's end today by meditating on a few scriptures. Read these over a few times and let God speak to you about them…

'Let everyone be quick to hear [be a careful, thoughtful listener], slow to speak [a speaker of carefully chosen words and], slow to anger [patient, reflective, forgiving]'
(James 1:19, AMP)

'But now rid yourselves [completely] of all these things: anger, rage, malice, slander, and obscene (abusive, filthy, vulgar) language from your mouth.' (Col. 3:8, AMP)

'Complain if you must, but don't lash out. Keep your mouth shut, and let your heart do the talking. Build your case before God and wait for his verdict.' (Psa. 4:4–5, *The Message*)

'**B**e not quick in your spirit to become angry, for anger lodges in the heart of fools.' (Eccl. 7:9)

The way to change your heart is to change your mind.

You may have heard it said that choosing not to forgive someone is like drinking poison and hoping the other person will die: it only causes you more pain.

God has given us the ability to forgive, in order to set us free to live the lives He has destined for us. Anger and peace cannot cohabit in our heart together; it is impossible.

One of my favourite verses is Isaiah 26:3, which says, 'You keep him in perfect peace whose mind is stayed on you, because he trusts in you.'

What would it look like for you to keep your mind 'stayed' (committed and focused) on the Lord? Are there things you need to do differently, habits you need to change or break?

Describe a time you felt in 'perfect peace' in your life (possibly when you first became a Christian, during a worship service, in a time of prayer). What were the circumstances surrounding it?

....

....

....

If 10 is perfect peace and 1 is anger and bitterness, where would you put your heart on that scale right now and why?

....

....

....

Summarise Colossians 3:12–15 in your own words. Think about the role peace plays in these verses.

....

....

....

....

....

End today by thanking God for His peace – a peace that goes beyond our understanding (Phil. 4:7) and is freely given to us by Christ (John 14:27).

Thursday

How many of you would like to receive a blessing and see good days in your life?

Yep, me too!

In 1 Peter 3:9–11, it says:

> 'Do not repay evil for evil or reviling for reviling, but on the contrary, bless, for to this you were called, that you may obtain a blessing. For "Whoever desires to love life and see good days, let him keep his tongue from evil and his lips from speaking deceit; let him turn away from evil and do good; let him seek peace and pursue it."'

Here, the apostle Peter is quoting David from Psalm 34:17–18, which goes on to say, 'When the righteous cry for help, the LORD hears and delivers them out of all their troubles. The LORD is near to the brokenhearted and saves the crushed in spirit.'

You may wonder why I'm focusing on peace, blessing and God's nearness when this week is about anger. It is because in my own life, I discovered anger was removed quicker when I chose to forgive and bless the one who hurt me, choosing intentionally to remain in God's peace. There is no quicker way to remove a mindset of anger than by choosing forgiveness and peace.

If you find there are still those who cause unrest to come in your spirit when you see or think of them, then I encourage you to pray the following prayer with me when you are ready:

Lord, I thank You for Your forgiveness in my life, which I received as a result of Jesus going to the cross for my sins. Jesus, I can never find enough words to thank You for the sacrifice You made on my behalf. I have carried unforgiveness and bitterness towards

_____

and I no longer want this seed lodged in my heart. I choose now to forgive _____ and release them to You. I ask that You will bless _____ and the desires of their heart. I release _____ from any debt owed to me and I choose now to receive peace, which goes beyond any understanding – a peace that only You can give. Thank You, Lord. Amen.

You may need to spend some time sitting and receiving that peace from God.

Chances are you may not feel any different in your heart toward that person straight away, and that's OK. As you continue daily praying blessing over them (do this intentionally, not because you feel like doing it!) you will slowly feel the hurt begin to subside and love replace anger.

As previously mentioned, we will eventually receive perfect peace when we choose to put our mind on Christ and walk in forgiveness toward others.

Friday

What a week! Well done for persevering and allowing the Holy Spirit to minister healing to your heart.

More than any other week, I encourage you today to review the entire past week's notes, scriptures and prayers, and see what else the Lord might want to say to you. Write what you hear from Him below.

....

....

....

....

....

....

....

....

....

....

Spend time imagining what it would look like, feel like and be like for you to spend an entire day in perfect – absolutely perfect – peace. Allow yourself to mediate on how it would be different from your normal day, *regardless* of circumstances or schedule. And ask the Holy Spirit what you can do now to help see that come to pass in your future.

. . . .

. . . .

. . . .

. . . .

. . . .

. . . .

Lord, thank You for holding my future in Your capable hands. Removing hurt and anger does not come from striving, but from spending time in Your presence. I choose to rest in Your peace and presence right now. Thank You for meeting me here and healing my heart, in time. Amen.

Part 2

The Truth

A GOD-GIVEN WAY
OF THINKING

Week 7

I am righteous

'He will bring forth your righteousness as the light, and your justice as the noonday.' (Psa. 37:6)

Monday

After spending several weeks wondering *'will my car start today?'*, my new battery and I were eagerly anticipating an anxiety-free journey to my next speaking engagement. The thought of starting it without apprehension felt too good to be true.

It was.

Turning the key and hearing the car start straightaway brought a momentary bubble of joy – soon to be popped when I looked at my dashboard to see the words:

Warning: Insufficient Oil Pressure.

You. Have. Got. To. Be. Kidding.

Six months away from the car being paid off and now this. Trying again, this time with the woeful sounds of 'Jesus pppllleeeaaassseee have mercy on my soul' filling the air, my car started and the warning light immediately faded into old news. *Phew,* I sighed, *that was close.*

But a few weeks later it popped up again, like annoying chin hair that seems to come from nowhere. (Really, God… *chin* hair?)

This time I used denial as my defence mechanism of choice: ignore it and it never happened.

Which worked brilliantly... for a while.

Then came the time I needed to make a 220 mile journey back to London from the South West. Hello, warning light. So I drove home as fast as I could, thinking if I drove really fast then I could possibly outrun the mechanical problem. (Admit it ladies, you've been there.)

After no change, I reluctantly took the car in for its yearly car service, mentioning it to the mechanic and dreading the cost that I was sure was to follow.

You see, it wasn't getting an upgrade that concerned me – it was the cost.

Have you ever found yourself in that position spiritually?

The 'cost' of following Christ and making Him your top priority seems too high... yet the choice of not paying that cost is higher.

It turned out that the cost was far less than expected and my parents had planned on sending me some money all along, so it was sorted and paid for at no extra cost to me.

This is what has been done for us spiritually. Your heavenly Father and His Son paid the ultimate cost of sacrifice, meaning anytime it's needed, you can receive your upgrade.

If you find yourself a bit low on 'oil' (time spent in His presence), look to see if you are responding as I did: pleading for mercy, living in denial or trying to outrun the warning signs.

None of these responses will bring the upgrade you need: they will only drain you further.

Instead, opt for an oil change.

And remember, no need to worry – the price has been paid.

Take a few minutes to meditate on the cost of following Christ. What has that looked like in your own life?

Tuesday

One of the key mindsets we need to get a revelation of – if we want to walk in freedom – is our righteousness in Christ, or we might say, our right-standing with God.

Righteousness comes through faith in Christ, by His grace, making us perfectly acceptable to a holy God, seen in His sight without blemish or blame.

One Greek definition says 'the state of him who is such as he ought to be'.[7] I love that. Being exactly as God originally created us to be.

The Bible also says we are 'seated… in the heavenly places in Christ Jesus' (Eph. 2:6) and that we 'have died and [our] life is now hidden with Christ in God' (Col. 3:3). The moment we make Jesus Lord of our life everything changes, we are a new creation (2 Cor. 5:17) and we have become the righteousness of God (2 Cor. 5:21). Outwardly all may look the same, but inwardly everything has changed.

Look up the above scriptures in your Bible and summarise in your own words what being righteous means to you.

In Philippians 3:9, it says that our righteousness 'depends on faith'. And we know that 'faith comes from hearing, and hearing through the word of Christ' (Rom. 10:17). So in order to keep a mindset of righteousness, we must continue in the Word of God – studying, hearing and speaking it regularly. We will not believe we are righteous if we do not continually remind ourselves and confess with our mouths that we are righteous.

Is this an easy thing for you to believe? If not, what makes it difficult?

....

....

....

You may need to review scriptures from the previous weeks in order to remove old mindsets before continuing to build a new mindset. If this seems difficult, then spend time meditating on today's scriptures, reading them aloud and declaring that you are a new creation, perfectly accepted by God and made holy by the blood of Christ... because you are!

Wednesday

I f I want to walk out my righteousness well, I must embrace His righteousness daily.

My righteousness is based on the righteousness of Christ; I am righteous *in Him*. And through this relationship, I have received every tool necessary to think on His truth and live in victory. There is no place in the Bible where a caveat is given for tough days, impossible situations or attacks from the enemy. Nowhere does it say to believe these things 'unless you are facing x, y, z'.

No, it says to believe and to obey what the Word says – regardless of what's happening around us. With that in mind, let's look at Matthew 6:33 (AMPC):

> 'But seek (aim at and strive after) first of all His kingdom and His righteousness (His way of doing and being right), and then all these things taken together will be given you besides.'

For us to see ourselves as righteous and to live as righteous, we need to keep His kingdom first in our hearts and minds. The Bible and our relationship with God must be the final authority over every circumstance and situation. It says that as we do that, He will take care of all other things in our lives. In other words, He does not want us worrying about 'these things', but instead we are to hand our circumstances and concerns over to Him, trusting in His loving care for us (1 Peter 5:7), and worshipping Him and His 'right-ness'.

Is there anything on your mind – or regularly taking up your thoughts – that you need to lay at the foot of the cross today?

. . . .

. . . .

. . . .

. . . .

In what ways have you changed by being a new creation in Christ?

. . . .

. . . .

. . . .

. . . .

Matthew 6:33 refers to earthly 'things' from verse 31, which lists examples such as food, drink and clothing. What else would go in your list, if those things are not your current point of concern? Will you choose to trust God with your specific cares?

. . . .

. . . .

. . . .

. . . .

Thursday

Remember on Monday we talked about an upgrade and 'oil' change? Today we are looking at several scriptures to kick-start that in a practical way.

Listed below are 15 scriptures from The Amplified Bible (Classic Edition) – which show what the life of a righteous person looks like according to Scripture. Each scripture has been summarised, and then in brackets you will find the beginning of a declaration you can use.

Take time to look them over, find them in your Bible and see which one(s) the Holy Spirit highlights to you. I encourage you to first read all the summaries out loud and then read all the declarations out loud. You will find your faith growing stronger the more you do this.

Psalm 1:6 – The Lord is acquainted with the way of the righteous. *(Lord, You are not absent, but are acquainted with my ways.)*

Psalm 5:12, Proverbs 10:6 – The Lord blesses the righteous. *(Lord, I receive Your blessings today.)*

Psalm 34:17, Proverbs 15:29 – When the righteous cry for help the Lord hears and delivers them. *(Lord, Your Word says You hear my prayers today and will deliver me.)*

Psalm 34:19 – Many evils confront the righteous, but the Lord delivers him from them all. *(Lord, You will deliver me from trouble when the enemy attacks me.)*

Psalm 64:10 – The righteous will be glad in the Lord, trust and take refuge in Him. *(Lord, I praise You and take refuge in You!)*

Psalm 92:12–15 – The righteous will flourish like the palm tree, long-lived, growing in grace and strength to old age. *(Lord, I will grow and bear fruit for You continually, even into my old age.)*

Psalm 146:8 – The Lord loves the righteous. *(Lord, I receive Your love.)*

Proverbs 3:32 – His confidential communion and secret counsel are with the righteous. *(Lord, I listen for Your secret counsel in my life right now.)*

Proverbs 12:13 – The righteous will come out of trouble. *(Lord, I thank You that this trouble will not last forever.)*

Proverbs 15:19 – The path of the righteous is raised and level. *(Lord, thank You for levelling the path in front of me.)*

Proverbs 24:16 – The righteous falls but rises again. *(Lord, thank You that when I stumble I will rise again.)*

Proverbs 28:1 – The righteous are as bold as a lion! *(Lord, I declare that I am as bold as a lion today!)*

James 5:16 – The prayer of the righteous one is powerful. *(Lord, I declare that my prayers are powerful today!)*

Friday

I t is not only reading the Word that sets us free, but *knowing* the Word. And like anything or anyone we want to get to know, we must study it.

So let's finish this week by studying some characteristics of the righteous person… Again, that's *you!*

The English Standard Version Bible titles Psalm 112 as 'The Righteous Will Never Be Moved'… I like that! As we have seen that we are the righteousness of God in Christ Jesus, let's take a look at some of the benefits that come with that standing.

These are benefits directly out of Psalm 112. Look it up in your Bible and find which verse contains the corresponding benefit. I've given you a sample here to get you started.

Benefits of the righteous woman:

Her offspring will be mighty in the land   verse 2

Wealth and riches are in her house

Light dawns in place of darkness

She will give generously and lend

She will conduct her affairs with justice

She will never be moved

She is not afraid of bad news

Her heart is firm, trusting in the Lord

Her heart is steady, she will not be afraid

She will look in triumph on her adversaries

She gives freely to the poor

Her righteousness will endure forever

What a list!

Finish today by thanking God for His goodness to you, making all of this available to you through His Son. Meditate on these truths more than on the negative circumstances around you, and you will begin to see a change in your outlook and attitude.

Week 8

I am honourable

'Love one another with brotherly affection.
Outdo one another in showing honor.'

(Rom. 12:10)

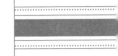

Monday

'We give honour to all men not just because they deserve it, but also because we are honourable citizens of the King.'[8]

This quote from Kris Vallotton sums up honour beautifully. In a world that loves to dishonour, expose, shame and compete, honour can stick out like a proverbial sore thumb. We are told to honour our parents, the Lord, our leaders and, according to the Apostle Peter, *everyone* (1 Pet. 2:17)!

Recently I tried to type the word 'self-centredness', yet when I looked at the screen I noticed auto-correct had changed it to 'self-centred mess'. Appropriate, no?! Self-centredness will always result in a mess, either now or in our future.

We cannot sow selfishness and expect to reap honour.

I've learned auto-correct is both a blessing and a frustration; how many times have we yelled at our smartphones saying 'I meant what I typed!'? If you've been in possession of your phone for more than five minutes, you've been there.

Or have you ever sent a text message and then realised that auto-correct had completely (and usually embarrassingly) changed your wording to something completely inappropriate?

One example I read recently said the following:

– You think he is the one?

– All I know is that he makes me really happy.
He's the only guy I've ever considered mutilating.

– … mutilating?!

– MARRYING!

While we joke about it and usually laugh it off, I think there is something we can glean from this spiritually.

Imagine we had someone with us who, each time we started to say something unkind or dishonouring, would turn our words into statements of encouragement and blessing. Or when we start to do something that could cause division, would step in and rearrange our effort to sow love and generosity. I can guess that many of us would love to have this in our own lives, saving us the grief of sinning and hurting others with our words and actions, reaping from our past mistakes. We could look amazing in front of everyone, be liked by all and reap blessings on the love we have sown.

In reality we *do* carry our own auto-correct with us at all times. His name is the Holy Spirit and He dwells within every believer, giving us counsel, assistance and letting us know what our Father is saying to us. And He is there to help us walk honourably, to auto-correct us by that still, small voice in our gut that says 'change your tone', 'bless them anyway', 'do not judge', 'forgive' etc…

When your instinct says 'dishonour' – regardless of the reason – auto-correct yourself. It is as simple as taking a few steps back and writing a different ending to that sentence, that thought or that gesture.

Then, and only then, SEND.

Take a few minutes to think if you have been a 'self-centred mess' recently. Is there anything you need to change, or someone you need to speak to, in order to make amends?

Tuesday

The word 'honour' is defined in the online Oxford dictionary as high respect; great esteem; the quality of knowing and doing what is morally right; something regarded as a rare opportunity and bringing pride and pleasure; a privilege.

We tend to use the word as a mark of respect to those in authority, or parental figures in our life, and as believers we seek to honour God in all that we do and say.

But have we allowed honour to become an actual *mindset* in our lives? Is it something we think about daily and seek to develop and maintain with everyone in our world and sphere of influence, or does it just 'happen' when it's a birthday or special celebration of someone in particular?

I believe it can become an intentional mindset that not only enriches the lives of those whom we are honouring, but our own lives as well.

Write below your own definition of honour. What does it mean or look like to you?

Now read the following two scriptures, written by the apostle Paul:

'So then, whether you eat or drink, or whatever you may do, do all for the honor *and* glory of God. Do not let yourselves be [hindrances by giving] an offense to the Jews or to the Greeks or to the church of God [do not lead others into sin by your mode of life]; Just as I myself strive to please [to accommodate myself to the opinions, desires, and interests of others, adapting myself to] all men in everything I do, not aiming at *or* considering my own profit *and* advantage, but that of the many in order that they may be saved. Pattern yourselves after me [follow my example], as I imitate *and* follow Christ (the Messiah).' (1 Cor. 10:31–11:1, AMPC)

'Now am I trying to win the favor of men, or of God? Do I seek to please men? If I were still seeking popularity with men, I should not be a bond servant of Christ (the Messiah).' (Gal. 1:10, AMPC)

These verses seem to contradict one another; in one Paul says that he pleases men in all things, and in the next verse he says he cannot live to please men or he wouldn't be a bond servant of Christ. Which is it?

Look at the scriptures surrounding these verses and then write your thoughts below. We will look at this in more detail tomorrow…

....

....

....

Wednesday

We left off yesterday with the (apparent) contradiction in Scripture about when to please people and when to please God.

At closer reading we see that in Galatians, Paul was specifically referring to those who would teach a gospel other than the Gospel of Christ. In that context, Paul declares he will not bow to the whims of man, in order to please them, over the conviction he held in Christ.

On the contrary, in 1 Corinthians 10 we see he is focused on unbelievers and Paul says he is willing to go to any lengths necessary to ensure they hear the good news of the gospel. There is no contradiction at all; they complement each other perfectly and give a good example of honouring both God and man.

Going back to the statement from Monday, we honour because *we* are honourable, not because the other person is honourable. God calls us to honour people as human beings, created in His image. Their behaviour may be anything but godly, yet their wrong behaviour does not permit us to walk in sin or judgment. We can judge the 'fruit' of their lives, but we cannot judge their hearts… only Jesus can do that.

There are many times we need to speak up for justice, and there are other times we should choose silence for wisdom's sake; only the Holy Spirit can reveal to you which is right for the situation.

But even in disagreement with others, it is still godly to keep a mindset and heart attitude of honour; choosing not to shame the person, while disagreeing with the action.

> 'It is to one's honour to avoid strife, but every fool is quick to quarrel.' (Prov. 20:3, NIVUK)

With all that in mind, ask the Holy Spirit to reveal if there is anyone in your life who you may have been judging incorrectly – or failing to show honour or respect to.

....

....

....

If anyone comes to mind, take time to repent for judging them and ask for God's blessing on their lives today, even if you are in disagreement with some choices they are making. Pray for breakthrough spiritually, that the blinkers would fall from their eyes and they would see how much they are loved by God.

....

....

....

Thursday

Jesus was intentionally honourable. Especially when it came to women – He honoured them by calling them 'daughter', healing them, speaking to them regardless of their cultural background and thinking of their needs even as He hung on a cross.

Similarly, once we know our freedom in Christ, we can stop looking solely to fulfil our own needs and can instead focus on meeting the needs of others. This is when it becomes really fun!

Who could you intentionally honour today and how? Try to think out of the box, someone you may not normally have interaction with, or a relationship that is encountering some struggles at the moment. Think of how Jesus sees them, and in light of that, how you can honour and bless them today.

....

....

....

The Message translates Proverbs 29:23 like this: 'Pride lands you flat on your face; humility prepares you for honors.'

By developing a mindset of honouring others instead of walking in judgment, we set ourselves up for a blessed life. It truly is much more fun to give than to receive! Yet we cannot out-give God, so as we honour others we will inevitably reap what we sow.

Honour must involve action. Jesus quoted the prophet Isaiah in Mark 7:6 when He said, 'This people honors me with their lips, but their heart is far from me'.

He was rebuking the Pharisees for their hypocritical practices and showing that words are meaningless if not attached to pure motives and sincere actions. Remember the auto-correct anecdote from Monday – 'self-centred mess'? That's what can happen if we disconnect the heart from the mouth when it comes to honour…

So, let me ask you again: who can you honour today and how?

....

....

....

....

....

Friday

Scripturally, it is impossible to separate renewing our mind and knowing God's will; the more we renew our mind to conform to His ways, the clearer His will for our lives will become.

> 'And do not be conformed to this world [any longer with its superficial values and customs], but be transformed and progressively changed [as you mature spiritually] by the *renewing of your mind* [focusing on godly values and ethical attitudes], so that you may prove [for yourselves] what the will of God is, that which is *good and acceptable and perfect* [in His *plan and purpose for you*].' (Rom. 12:2, AMP, emphasis mine)

And one of the benefits of walking in a renewed mindset is the desire to bless others instead of striving to obtain blessings for ourselves.

Philippians 2:4 says, 'Let each of you look not only to his own interests, but also to the interests of others.'

Note that it doesn't say to ignore your own interests! It says *in addition to your interests*, look out for the interests of others. So this isn't a self-effacing humility that never looks to her own needs or desires, but one which balances it with the benefit to others.

Take some time to consider how you handle that balance, and allow the Holy Spirit to reveal if there is any imbalance in your life around honour.

....

....

....

....

....

....

....

Then pray through it, reviewing the scriptures of this week, committing yourself again to 'take every thought captive to obey Christ' (2 Cor. 10:5), seeking to intentionally honour others with your thoughts, words and actions.

Week 9

I am joy-filled

'Then our mouth was filled with laughter,

and our tongue with shouts of joy;

then they said among the nations,

"The Lord has done great things for them."

The Lord has done great things for us;

we are glad.' (Psa. 126:2–3)

Monday

My friend was busy in the kitchen, so I thought I'd grab a few moments playing with her four-year-old son in the lounge. As I peered into the room, I noticed he was a bit 'lost in space', so I left him alone and went back into the kitchen.

After a while he came shuffling in to see what we were up to. I mentioned seeing him 'zoning out' earlier, to which he flatly replied, 'that was my medium face.'

I looked to his mum for an explanation.

Through laughter she explained that recently she and her husband had noticed Noah looking a bit adrift, so they questioned if he was alright. He nonchalantly said, 'I'm fine; this is my medium face.' As they looked understandably confused, he explained to them he wasn't very happy, nor was he very sad; he was… medium.

Aside from the obvious profundity for a child, I find his expression remarkably accurate. He was right! His face was not particularly joyful, nor was it painfully sour; if it was coffee it would have been level three intensity – medium.

This got me thinking: Does joy have to be shown in an abundance of teeth, laughter and hilarity? Can we be quietly joyful? Is it possible to have deep-seated joy while sporting a medium face?

I believe it is. Because joy is a fruit of the Spirit, which Jesus walked in perfectly, yet I don't sense from Scripture that He had a cheesy grin on His face 24/7. He had to be the most joy-filled man to ever walk the earth, but a quick glance at the concordance will show you remarkably few verses in the Gospels that include the word 'joy' in reference to Christ or His life. Far more is said throughout the rest of the New Testament, particularly in some of Paul's writings where he had learned to rejoice regardless of what was happening to or around him.

Nearing the end of His life, Jesus said these words: 'These things I have spoken to you, that my joy may be in you, and that your joy may be full' (John 15:11). Here it is clear that joy is something innate, not something manufactured; it is reflected, and not prescribed.

As much as I wanted little Noah to smile and play like a four-year-old 'should', in reality he was completely at peace and enjoying himself just as he was, resting in the moment.

I imagine Jesus like that: looking into the distance as He sits with His disciples, thinking of those He loves, joking around with the little children, chatting to His Father, healing the sick – all done full of joy… while, at times, wearing His 'medium face'.

How would you define joy in your life today?

....

....

....

....

....

....

Lord, help me to know Your joy, regardless of my circumstances. Thank You that I can be real with You, whatever I'm feeling. Amen.

Tuesday

J oy is your heritage as a child of God.

It's not dependent on circumstances, finances, health or any other material or positional blessing. It is a gift given to us when we receive the Spirit (Gal. 5:22). In Nehemiah, we are told not to lose hope, 'for the *joy* of the LORD *is your strength*' (Neh. 8:10, emphasis mine). I love this version because in my Bible it emphasises the word 'LORD' by capital letters.

An important sidenote: When reading the Bible, have you ever noticed the variations of 'Lord' and 'LORD'? There is actually a significant reason for these differences. In the Old Testament, 'Lord' appears as the translation of 'Adonai', a name of God that emphasises His lordship and authority. 'LORD' however, is the translation of God's Hebrew name 'YHWH', the holiest of God's holy names. Nobody actually knows how to pronounce 'YHWH' – partly because there were no vowels in the written Ancient Hebrew alphabet, and partly because this name of God was so holy that it was forbidden to speak it out loud. Scholars state their closest guesses as 'Jehovah / Yahweh / Yehowah'. It could be something different – we simply don't know, which is why LORD is used.

Joy is not synonymous with happiness; it is a fruit of the Spirit coming from YHWH Himself, containing 'supernatural' strength to go beyond 'natural' circumstances. The 'Unspeakable Name', uttered by a spirit in praise, creates an unceasing flow of pure joy that is ours for the receiving, releasing His strength into our sorrow.

'Joy' found in circumstances, changes with them. However, true joy found in Jesus Christ – who embodies the Spirit of the Sovereign Lord (Luke 4:18) – is like Him: the same. Yesterday. Today. And forever (Heb. 13:8).

How does that thought make you feel about your current circumstances? Take some time to think about your life right now; are you able to experience and reflect joy – regardless of what is or is not happening to you or around you?

. . . .

. . . .

. . . .

I would encourage you to read the whole of Nehemiah 8. In it, Ezra is reading the Book of the Law of Moses to a people who had not heard these words for a very long time, due to exile. Their hearts were stirred and they began to weep at hearing the Scriptures once more. If you have been away from the Lord, or put up a wall out of anger or disappointment, then once the Word is spoken you may begin to feel emotional as your spirit is refreshed. But Ezra encouraged them not to weep, instead to rejoice in the joy they receive from the Lord.

Are you weeping when God is asking you to rejoice? Have you gotten into a habit of seeing the negative over the positive?

Wednesday

We finished yesterday by considering how to choose joy over sorrow.

Because, as much as this frustrates me sometimes, the truth is: *joy is my choice!*

1 Thessalonians 5:16 says to 'Rejoice always…'

Philippians 4:4 says to 'Rejoice in the Lord always…'

Colossians 3:15 says to 'be thankful'.

James 1:2 says to 'Count it all joy…'

God would never have allowed these words to be written if they were impossible to execute, and He certainly wouldn't have said 'always' if it was dependent on our circumstances.

But we cannot do this in our own strength; it must be intentional and done by faith in the Word of God, which says that joy is *already* in us through the Holy Spirit in us (Gal. 5:22–25)! We simply choose to meditate on it, allowing it to grow stronger, finally seeing its evidence through our thoughts and actions.

Look up today's verses and say them out loud over your life. Declare that *'I am joyful always... I rejoice always... I am thankful... I do count it all joy!'* Repeat this as many times as necessary to begin to feel your faith rise in this area. It truly is good medicine for your soul!

Write out Proverbs 17:22 below as a reminder.

....

....

....

Let's finish by returning to yesterday's verse from Nehemiah.

Ellicott's Commentary for English Readers says this about Nehemiah 8:10: 'This beautiful sentence is, literally, *delight in Jehovah is a strong refuge.* It is capable of unlimited application in preaching and devotion.'[9]

Now take time to meditate on the truth that delighting in Him creates a strong refuge for whatever you might be facing, for the unlimited amount of times you might need it.

Thursday

Joy is not solely for our own enjoyment. Nor is it only for our strengthening. Joy allows us to think beyond our circumstances to the needs of others, giving to others where we may have need ourselves, and finding that in doing so… we gain even greater joy.

Once again, let's visit Nehemiah 8:10.

Ezra tells the people to 'send portions to anyone who has nothing ready'… in other words, give to the one in need.

To a world that often connects joy with receiving, we live from a different kingdom that says *real* joy is found in giving.

Hebrews 12:2 says, 'who for the joy that was set before him endured the cross'. Jesus endured horrific circumstances because His gaze was fixed on something far greater than that moment — you and I. We are His joy! *Us* living in perpetual joy through the Holy Spirit was the image that Jesus kept in front of Him as He endured pain beyond anything we can imagine.

Take a few minutes to simply THANK HIM for that!

Jesus, we worship You! We thank You for the cross, thank You for what You endured to save us, free us and bring us into relationship with You. Thank You for the *joy* we walk in right now because of what You chose to endure. We can never thank You enough – but I choose now to worship You as Lord of Lords, and as Lord over my life and circumstances!

Ahh, that feels good doesn't it?! Regardless of what I am walking through right now, I can praise Him because He is so good and has taken my sin and punishment for all of eternity. If I receive nothing else in this lifetime, I still have reason to rejoice!

Because we have received this amazing gift, how much more should we give to others?

Ask the Holy Spirit who you can bless today and how.

. . . .

. . . .

. . . .

Finally, meditate on today's scriptures. Get them in your mind, heart and spirit, as that is the way you will walk in true victory.

Friday

Imagine you were stuck in prison with hardly any daylight, no running water, no toilet, chains around your ankles, flimsy clothing in winter and a pungent sewage smell as your constant companion.

John McRay wrote it this way in *Christianity Today*:

'Roman imprisonment was preceded by being stripped naked and then flogged, a humiliating, painful, and bloody ordeal. The bleeding wounds went untreated; prisoners sat in painful leg or wrist chains. Mutilated, blood-stained clothing was not replaced, even in the cold of winter... Most cells were dark, especially the inner cells of a prison, like the one Paul and Silas inhabited in Philippi. Unbearable cold, lack of water, cramped quarters, and sickening stench from few toilets made sleeping difficult and waking hours miserable.'[10]

And it was in these conditions that the Apostle Paul wrote the book of Philippians, in which he quoted 'joy', 'rejoice' or 'rejoiced' between 15 and 19 times (depending on your source) in only four chapters.

Clearly joy was not dependent on circumstances; *it was a choice.*

A mindset.

A truth which, if we allow, can transform our thoughts, conversations and lifestyles.

As we finish this week, take time to review the scriptures we have read.

Remember that contentment is not the result of receiving an answer, but the response that comes from knowing the one who is *the* answer.

Lord, once again I thank You for enduring pain to give me joy. I choose to walk in the joy I already have through the fruit of the Spirit, and I declare my life will reflect the joy I have in knowing I am saved, redeemed, freed and blessed as Your child. I choose joy! Amen.

Week 10

I am at peace

'Yes, my soul, find rest in God;

my hope comes from him.' (Psa. 62:5, NIVUK)

Monday

'I have never had clarity; what I have always had is trust. So I will pray that you will trust God.' – Mother Teresa[11]

Walking through a difficult season, I came across this quote and it quickly gave me perspective.

On and off for months I had been praying for clarity, asking God what He was doing, when things would change and why He was allowing me to hurt so deeply. If only there was an answer, then I could bear up under the weight of disappointment, frustration and confusion.

But as is often the case with God, His answer was not what I had been expecting.

It reminds me of a date I went on many years ago…

This happened during the early days of internet dating when it was still a bit taboo, but being in your late thirties and never married will challenge one's ideal of how to meet 'the one'. So this potential partner travelled to Devon, where I was living, to stay with his sister so we could meet up to get to know one another better.

About an hour after boarding the train for home, he phoned me (which I thought was a good start) and began saying how much he enjoyed our time together (yay, Lord!), that he thought I was great (holding breath here), amazing even (score!)… and that it made him realise he wanted to get back with his ex-girlfriend.

Insert awkward silence.

All the signs had led me to a different conclusion than the one I actually received.

I was finally amazing… but apparently that still wasn't good enough. I expected one outcome yet I received another.

Maybe you've also experienced this in life. The job seemed perfect, the man ticked all the boxes or the home was everything you had dreamed of… until suddenly it wasn't.

What do you do when life seems to fall apart? Where do you find peace amidst a storm of question marks and confusion?

Mother Teresa had obviously been there and the lesson she learned gives us fresh perspective to painful truths.

It isn't clarity we should be seeking; it is trust we should be developing.

As new Christians, we need God to provide clarity for our lives, speaking clearly and reminding us He is there. But as we mature, He asks us to trust Him for who He is and not only for what He does. Because in doing so, we walk out of self-centredness (or our 'self-centred mess') and into biblical maturity.

Quite simply, it is in the minimising of clarity that the maximising of trust is established.

Amazing.

Lord, at the beginning of this week, I take the time now to rest in Your presence and to receive Your peace. Amen.

Tuesday

'In returning and rest you shall be saved; in quietness and in trust shall be your strength' (Isa. 30:15).

We have spent many weeks changing our mindsets from negative to life-giving, and we will continue this week by looking at 'peace'.

But before we go there, let's camp for a quick minute on the word 'trust'. Most of us have anxiety because we are unsure or fearful about the outcome of a situation, but as we saw yesterday from Mother Teresa, trust is critical to living a life of peace.

The answer is not my goal; relationship with my Lord is the goal (Matt. 6:33; Prov. 3:5–6). As I seek Him, meditate on His Word and enjoy His blessings, then all other things will be added to me. But we often want the latter before the former; we desire to see the result and then we will come to Him in thanksgiving!

Think about how much you trust the Lord right now. Be honest. If there are areas you are struggling with, hold them before Him in prayer, asking the Holy Spirit to help you release them to the one who fashioned the stars in the skies and holds the planets in His hands.

If you struggle to do this, I encourage you to read today's scriptures in Isaiah, Matthew and Proverbs several times out loud, letting the truth increase your faith, which will in turn, build your trust.

Now let's pray some declarations over our lives for this week, believing that God is who He says He is, and will do what He says He will do!

Lord, I declare you are good. I declare you are faithful. And I declare You are love. I rest in Your goodness, faithfulness and love right now where I am in life, and I trust You with the concerns on my heart. I declare Your eye is on me and that You are holding me in the palm of Your hand and in the centre of Your heart. I declare I will trust You today, regardless of my circumstances, knowing that Your Word says You desire to bless me richly (Prov. 10:22). Amen.

Wednesday

Yesterday we declared our trust in God. If this is still an area of struggle for you, then I encourage you to review yesterday's scriptures over and over until your faith begins to build in that area. Don't rush this; it's fine if you aren't on the correct day of the week!

One of my favourite verses is Romans 15:13, which says, 'May the God of hope fill you with all joy and peace as you trust in him, so that you may overflow with hope by the power of the Holy Spirit' (NIVUK).

I also like the New Living Translation, which puts it this way: 'I pray that God, *the source of hope*, will fill you completely with joy and peace *because you trust in him*. Then you will overflow with confident hope through the power of the Holy Spirit' (emphasis mine).

Notice how trust is the foundation upon which hope, joy and peace is built. If you have a shaky foundation, you will have an unstable structure.

You might be saying at this point, 'I thought this week was about peace and all you've done is talk about trust?' Very observant! And accurate. You see, I have found in my own life that 'striving after peace' is an oxymoron that produces little result.

Psalm 46:10 in the NASB says, 'Cease striving and know that I am God'.

Striving never produces peace.

So if we are 'trying' to get peace, then we have already started on the wrong foot and with an incorrect motive. Peace is in us (Gal. 5:22) and simply needs to be cultivated, through trust, in a God who gives hope.

Below each of the *incredible* promises found in Romans 15:13 (NLT), write how you have seen them outworked in your own life.

God is the source.

....

Trust is the foundation.

....

Hope is the conduit.

....

Joy and peace are the life-flow.

....

The Holy Spirit is the power.

....

Confidence is the result.

....

Thursday

To me, *shalom* is a truly beautiful Hebrew word. We often think of it in reference to peace – but it is so much more than that.

Here is a more thorough definition:

'The root denotes completion or wholeness. The general meaning of the root word is of entering into a state of wholeness and unity, a restored relationship. It also conveys a wide range of nuances: fulfillment, completion, maturity, soundness, wholeness, harmony, tranquillity, security, wellbeing, welfare, friendship, agreement, success and prosperity.'[12]

Isaiah 26:3 says, 'You keep him in perfect peace [*shalom*] whose mind is stayed on you, because he trusts in you' (square brackets mine).

The Complete Jewish Bible puts it this way: 'A person whose desire rests on you, you preserve in perfect peace [shalom], because he trusts in you'.

I like that: 'whose desire rests on You'.

Where does your desire rest – really rest – today?

If we are trusting in anything other than the security found in Christ, we are on shaky ground. If our identity is found in our spouse, children, job, position, title, image, wealth, ministry or 'successes', then we live a life without true security.

As the well-known song says:

'My hope is built on nothing less
Than Jesus' blood and righteousness;
I dare not trust the sweetest frame,
But wholly lean on Jesus' name.
On Christ, the solid Rock, I stand;
All other ground is sinking sand.'[13]

Is there anything today keeping you from trusting wholly on the solid rock of Christ? If so, write it below and spend time in prayer holding it before God. (Phone a friend to pray with you if this is an area that is particularly difficult.) *Always* pray from the perspective that God is good, and that His desire is to bless you, as that is the truth from the Word.

....

....

....

....

....

....

Friday

We've seen this week that peace needs a foundation of trust, and that it has nothing whatsoever to do with our circumstances. It is the fruit of the Spirit of God within us, a gift we did not earn and one we cannot lose.

What have you learned, or been reminded of, as you've meditated on peace this week?

. . . .

. . . .

. . . .

. . . .

. . . .

Let's conclude this week by reading the words of Jesus.

In John 14:27, Jesus says 'Peace I leave with you; my peace I give to you. Not as the world gives do I give to you. Let not your hearts be troubled, neither let them be afraid.'

Looking again at the Complete Jewish Bible we see the word 'shalom': 'What I am leaving with you is *shalom* — I am giving you my *shalom*. I don't give the way the world gives. Don't let yourselves be upset or frightened' (emphasis mine).

Chapters 14–17 of John's Gospel are known as the Farewell Discourse, as they are Jesus' last words before His public life comes to an end. As with anyone who knows death is imminent, last words are carefully chosen.

Jesus would not give us what we could not keep.

But He never meant us to keep it by our own effort.

In staying connected to Him, empowered by Holy Spirit, we can let this fruit grow to the point where anxiety and the cares of this world are thrown onto Him, leaving us in the 'shalom-peace' He intended.

Thank You Jesus for Your sacrifice, which brings my peace. I choose Your peace over my anxiety and I release my cares to You today. I will meditate and think on peace any time anxiety tries to surface. I receive perfect peace from You today! Amen.

Week 11

I am His friend

'One who has unreliable friends soon comes to ruin, but there is a friend who sticks closer than a brother.' (Prov. 18:24, NIVUK)

Monday

His name was Mexico.

He had a sombrero, was about three feet tall with black hair and always wore a sweet smile on his face. A gentle soul, he would follow me around and always be there whenever I looked for him. In my own childlike way, I loved him.

Yet, he was invisible to everyone except me.

Surely I'm not the only one who had an imaginary friend as a young child?

It's quite common for kids to have imaginary friends because they have not yet learned to stifle their creativity in place of the more restrained, logical thinking that the world often esteems over imagination.

Children don't yet know that the unseen can be viewed as wrong, and the illogical as messy, until proven factual. They simply let their creativity flow and enjoy whatever bubbles to the surface in that moment… it's beautiful to watch… and sad to see go.

Granted, if I was still speaking to Mexico on a regular basis today, I would encourage you to have me see a professional. Talking to figments of our imagination is not a typically accepted practice in today's society – and for good reason, I might add.

Yet I wonder if we have allowed that to seep into our Christian life as well?

Sure, we pray, and some are more comfortable praying out loud than others, but we don't walk around speaking to Jesus like He's actually standing right next to us. Because of course He's seated in heaven, so how ludicrous to expect He'd enjoy sitting at our kitchen table…

And yet, He does.

He is far from imaginary; rather, He is very present and with us wherever we go. He is always available. Because He's our friend, and that's what friends do.

Friends are there for you when you need them; they laugh at your jokes and cry when you grieve. They lift up your hands and they give when you have need. They aren't too busy and they don't go absent for no reason; they stay connected, no matter how difficult.

In John 15, Jesus calls us His friends. What an honour. *Friends of God.* I think perhaps we have become so used to that phrase that we've misplaced the awe of our standing… on a first-name basis with the creator of the universe. If we were good friends with the Prime Minister we'd want everyone to know, yet do we boast in the same measure about our friendship with God?

I grew out of Mexico's friendship, and rightly so, but I can still picture him in my mind's eye. I like to believe it was my heavenly Father's way of letting me know that even though I experienced some painful experiences as a child, I was never alone.

Maybe he wasn't so imaginary after all.

How comfortable are you with the thought of Jesus sitting at your kitchen table with you? What would you say to Him?

....

....

....

....

....

....

....

....

As we are tackling mindsets in this devotional, I want to remind you of Week Four, which we ended with the knowledge that we can *never* be alone if we are a believer. The Father, Son and Holy Spirit are with us 24/7 and, in fact, the Spirit dwells *within* us… you cannot get much closer than that!

From many conversations and times of prayer ministry with people, I find that we tend to be more comfortable with one of the Trinity than with the others. Some find themselves able to relate more easily to the Father, some to the Son and still others to the Holy Spirit.

Who would you say you are most comfortable with? (There's no right or wrong answer.) Has this changed for you over the years?

....

....

....

....

I found in my early days as a Christian that I was scared of the Father, I didn't understand the Holy Spirit, but I could trust Jesus. So He quickly became my best friend, and I talked to Him about everything. In fact, as a 20-something Christian girl, I remember taking walks with Him, holding His hand, enjoying the fact that nobody else knew Jesus was on the other side of my closed fist!

To some this may sound a bit heretical, but I am convinced this built a very strong foundation of trust and love on which I still stand today. Of course I knew Jesus wasn't physically standing there – He's next to His Father in heaven – but I also knew He didn't mind me imagining Him beside me.

One day I was walking with Him and as I veered a bit to the left to avoid a mud puddle, I looked down to realise it left 'Him' in the very middle of it. I laughed and apologised. Instantly in my spirit, not audibly, I heard the words 'Jen, I've walked on water before!'

I laughed, clutched my hand tighter and continued walking with my friend.

How would you describe your friendship with Jesus (or the Father/Holy Spirit)?

....

....

....

....

Lord, help me to know You as my friend. I pray that even this week we will experience a renewed sense of love, joy and friendship in our relationship. Amen.

Wednesday

Before we go further into this week's study, let me clarify: I am not advocating a non-honouring, on-my-level, 'buddy' type relationship with the creator of the universe!

He is God, and we must always respect, acknowledge and honour Him for that. In no way do I think a nonchalant, casual relationship is appropriate. That isn't what I am saying.

Rather, I am intending to illustrate that He is not just sitting high up on His throne, uninterested in the 'little people' down below, moving us around like puppets for His own personal gain. Sadly, Christians have vacillated between these two images over the years.

He is not uninvolved – but nor is He my equal.

With that in mind, let's look at John 15:15 (NIVUK): 'I no longer call you servants, because a servant does not know his master's business. Instead, I have called you friends, for everything that I learned from my Father I have made known to you.'

He was saying that all He had taught up to this point was now open as revelation to them; all that the Father taught Him, He then taught His disciples.

What are some of the benefits you have received from a friendship with your creator?

....
....
....
....

What are some of the greatest lessons you've learned through having a friendship with Him?

....
....
....
....

Tell Him, in your own words, what His friendship means to you.

....
....
....
....
....
....
....

Thursday

I n Exodus 33:11, it says that the Lord used to 'speak to Moses face to face, *as a man speaks to his friend*' (emphasis mine). Imagine that!

We know from Scripture that Moses had a very special relationship with God. He was chosen to lead the Israelites out of Egypt, climb the mountain to record the Ten Commandments, and on God's word, to part the Red Sea, just to name a few of Moses' tasks! There was a trust relationship between them that was beautiful, and that grew over time. Moses had his moments of doubt (needing Aaron as his mouthpiece and hitting the rock in a temper tantrum come to mind) but overall, his friendship with God remained strong.

And one of the reasons why I believe it did was his intentionality.

He *intentionally* spent time in God's presence, sought His counsel and obeyed His laws.

Let's pause here for reflection.

Without stepping into unnecessary guilt, think about your time with God and assess how much time you spend in His presence, seeking His counsel and walking in obedience to His Word.

Is there anything the Holy Spirit is highlighting to you as an area to look at and change?

. . . .

. . . .

. . . .

In Exodus 32 we read about the Israelites creating an idol in the image of a golden calf. This was done after getting tired of waiting for an answer from God. They decided it would be better to take matters into their own hands instead of trusting God to lead them.

Delay is a test that leads us toward devotion or disaster; the choice is ours. Any idols in our lives will keep us from a deeper friendship with God. He wants – rightly so – no other gods before Him.

Let's finish today by asking the Holy Spirit if there are any idols keeping you from drawing nearer to God. Write below what you hear.

. . . .

. . . .

. . . .

Lord, I desire You above all else. I long to grow closer to You and I am excited to know You in a way this year that I didn't know You last year. Whether this comes through trial or triumph, I ask that You would draw near to me as I draw near to You. I love You as much as I'm able right now; please expand my heart to love You even deeper tomorrow. You are my joy. Amen.

Friday

'Greater love has no one than this, that someone lay down his life for his friends.' (John 15:13)

Someone laid down His life for yours.

He took your place. Received your punishment. Accepted your sin, sickness and disease.

Three times in John 21, Jesus asks Peter if he loves Him. And three times Peter affirms that He does.

Jesus didn't need the reassurance; Peter needed the declaration. He needed to hear himself say what he truly believed – that he loved Jesus, deeply.

So let's finish this week by writing a love letter to your greatest friend, Jesus. This may be new to you; don't worry, there is absolutely no right or wrong way to do this. It can be two lines long or it can be a novel.

Use the rest of the space here (or more in another journal if you like) to record a love letter to your Saviour – thanking Him for His sacrifice, declaring your love for Him and accepting the role of 'friend' with Him, as we have seen today in John 15. Enjoy!

Week 12

I am His servant

'But I do not account my life of any value nor as precious to myself, if only I may finish my course and the ministry that I received from the Lord Jesus, to testify to the gospel of the grace of God.' (Acts 20:24)

Monday

One of the most picturesque places in England (and the world) is found on the southern edge of Devon. Though its label 'The English Riviera' may be a tad ambitious, to me this tiny fishing town is the equivalent of warm custard on a cold winter's day. Brixham is where I head when I need 'home' this side of the Atlantic. It's where I find solace, reconnecting with a lifestyle of peace and of what's important.

One particular day, I was in desperate need of 'Jen time' so I ventured out to the cliffs, anticipating a quiet cream tea and a stunning seaside view.

After walking for a while, I found a café and soon I was sat outside with a hot latte and a warm scone, remembering what air tastes like outside of London. I enjoyed the sound of seagulls and smiled at the warm sun on my face.

This was a perfect morning with a perfect view. And... relax.

Cue: two old men lumbering up to the very wall over which I was gazing, completely blocking my view.

With my not-very-Christian glare deftly hidden behind my sunglasses, I bemoaned the perfect view lost to a couple of old men having a jolly chat.

Reluctantly, I moved. Walking further down the hill I found another bench. In front of it was a sharp cliff with a steep incline – blocking my view now would cause them serious damage. With a deep sigh I smiled, feeling victorious and content once again.

Cue: a noise. Looking directly behind me was – you guessed it – one of the old men, who had come over to evangelise me, desperate for my soul to be saved. Once assured that I was bound for heaven, things changed – he handed over his business card, wished me well and promised to leave me alone. Thank You, Jesus.

Sunglasses back on, and… solitude.

But now I couldn't rest.

It struck me that not once had I thought about anyone else at the café that morning. I was so annoyed at the obstruction, I wasn't open to an invitation.

Even if God had wanted to speak to me about anyone there, I was too self-obsessed to hear Him. All I wanted was some space – was that too much to ask?

Jesus understood. In Matthew 14:13–14, we read how He needed peace and solitude, only to find a waiting crowd upon arriving at His own seaside retreat. Being Jesus, His attitude was much better than mine.

He welcomed the crowd, ministered healing to the hurting and proceeded to feed over 5,000 of them from a bit of bread and a few fish. He was interrupted by thousands and I was annoyed at two.

If I call myself a servant of Christ, I exist to serve an audience of one.

Of course it isn't too much to ask for time away – Jesus did that regularly – but I must never let my me-time hide me from what is most important to the heart of God in the moment… which may be two jolly old men sitting on a wall.

Do you have a particular room or chair where you go to 'get away from it all' with the Lord? If not, I would encourage you to find a special place to meet with Him regularly.

Tuesday

W e are nearing the end of our time together – the final week!

Over the past 12 weeks we have looked at mindsets that hold us back, ones that need removing and others that need improving. We have discovered the truth of the Word, the power of declaration and the deepening of our relationship with the creator.

So in this final week, I want us to look at a mindset of service.

Thus far it has been mostly about us, but now we are shifting gears. As we read a few days ago in John 15:15, Jesus has called us friends. But it does not end there.

He goes on to challenge us to ask whatever we want in His name, to stand strong against persecution, to welcome the help of Holy Spirit and to stand unified as we take this truth into the world (John 15:15–17). In other words, *it's not all about me.*

So, before we go any further this week, let's go back to the scripture mentioned yesterday: Matthew 14:13–21. We read in verse 15 that the disciples say to Jesus, 'This is a *desolate* place, and the day is now *over'* (emphasis mine). In other words, the place and time are not appropriate for a miracle.

Have you ever thought that? 'Because of *x, y, z,* I don't see God able to fix this situation.'

In reality, the disciples were thinking more about themselves than they were the crowds. How were they going to feed them all? Impossible! Therefore the only solution was to send them away hungry.

To a Saviour with the ear of His Father, this was simply unacceptable.

Is there any situation you feel tempted to push away because it looks impossible, the timing feels wrong or the people seem inappropriate?

....

....

....

....

Holy Spirit, please bring to mind any person or situation I have tried to take into (or dismiss from) my own hands, instead of trusting Yours. Thank You for showing me the way forward. Amen.

Wednesday

The miracle in Matthew 14 happened when the disciples handed out the bread.

Jesus allowed their hands to touch the impossible and see the unimaginable.

He loves to partner with us in that way. Remember Moses used *his* staff to part the Red Sea, the Israelites used *their* voices to shout down the wall in Jericho, Peter stretched out *his* hand and helped raise Dorcas from the dead…

You are a vital part of God's plan and He desires to use your hands, voice and resources to restore a broken world back to Himself.

How does that make you feel?

....

....

....

....

'I have been crucified with Christ; it is no longer I who live, but Christ lives in me' (Gal. 2:20).

What does this verse mean to you personally? What does this truth look like for you?

....

....

....

....

....

The evangelist Oswald Chambers interpreted Galatians 2:20 as follows:

> 'These words mean the breaking and collapse of my independence brought about by my own hands, and the surrendering of my life to the supremacy of the Lord Jesus. No one can do this for me, I must do it myself. God may bring me up to this point 365 times a year, but He cannot push me through it. It means breaking the hard outer layer of my individual independence from God, and the liberating of myself and my nature into oneness with Him; not following my own ideas, but choosing absolute loyalty to Jesus. Once I am at that point, there is no possibility of misunderstanding.'[14]

Do you find this difficult? In what ways?

....

....

....

....

Thursday

It's a privilege to partner.

This is perfectly modelled for us in the Trinity – Father, Son, Spirit as one – working seamlessly together, complementing one another and bringing about far more together than one could do alone. In fact, our Christian walk wouldn't work without this perfect unity.

Yet at one point it wasn't perfect.

Because we weren't yet part of the story.

You have a vital role to play in God's plan for humanity, whether you are 15 or 105; if you are breathing, you have purpose. In this season of your life, what do you feel is the best way you can serve the Lord?

In 1 Corinthians 9:24–27, we read how Paul looked at his own life as a servant. He says, 'Do you not know that in a race all the runners run, but only one receives the prize? So run that you may obtain it. Every athlete exercises self-control in all things. They do it to receive a perishable wreath, but we are imperishable. So

I do not run aimlessly; I do not box as one beating the air. But I discipline my body and keep it under control, lest after preaching to others I myself should be disqualified.'

Several years ago I was speaking at an event, and in the midst of my talk I said, 'We need to make a decisive decision…' and everyone laughed. Only then did I realise that any decision, by definition, is decisive!

What I was trying to get across was the point of making a firm and immovable decision. This is what Paul is referring to 1 Corinthians. You can hear in the language that he is not messing around; he is determined to run a good race and will do whatever is necessary to win!

Are you?

Is there anything keeping you from throwing aside current entanglements and running the road marked in front of you with greater perseverance?

....

....

....

Take time praying and declaring your desire to run well and to be used by God for His purposes in your life during this season.

Friday

Y ou've made it!

I have intentionally included a plethora of scriptures throughout this book, knowing that faith comes by hearing and hearing by the Word of God.

And in order for mindsets to change, we must replace the negative thinking that lines up with the world, with the truth that lines up with the kingdom of God.

A kingdom mindset is a mind obedient to the King.

And a mind obedient to the King makes one… unstoppable.

Take time to review the pages in the book, read what you have written, observe the progress you have made and record any particular chapter(s) you may want to revisit.

....

....

....

....

....

Mindsets take time to change, and the key to breakthrough will be intentionality and consistency. God has already done His part. He has given us the mind of Christ; we carry the Holy Spirit within us to help; and we have the Word at our fingertips to speak out of our mouths and get deep in our hearts as often as we like.

Change will come as we choose differently.

Find scriptures that come alive to you and write them out, stick them on your mirror or in the notes section at the back of this book, and repeat them until you believe them!

This is a journey that never ends – it only gets more fun the further you go!

Let's end with a blessing and a declaration…

Lord, I (Jen) bless each woman who has put her mind and heart towards finishing this study. She is Your chosen daughter and You adore her! I declare right now that her future is greater than her past, that her best is yet to come, that as she fixes her eyes on You whom she cannot see, there will be a shift in the circumstances that she can see. I declare a new confidence, a strong voice and a gentle spirit to guide her into tomorrow and her next season. Break open Your anointing over her and shower her with blessings too many to count. And we give You all the glory for it, forever. Amen!

Notes

Notes

Notes

Endnotes

[1] Michael Hyatt, 'The Gift of Validation', 02/02/2009, taken from www.michaelhyatt.com

[2] Cambridge Bible, taken from www.biblehub.com/commentaries

[3] Rev Dr Mary Caygill, 'The Politics of Compassion, Part 2: Mark 7:24–30', Pentecost 15 – 06 September 2015, www.durhamstreetmethodist.wordpress.com

[4] Steven Furtick (@stevenfurtick), 'One reason we struggle w/ insecurity: we're comparing our behind the scenes to everyone else's highlight reel.' Twitter post: 10/05/2011, 8.58am

[5] Guy Winch PhD, The Squeaky Wheel, '10 Surprising Facts About Loneliness', Psychology Today post: 21/10/2014, taken from www.psychologytoday.com/blog

[6] Joyce Meyer, *The Root of Rejection* (Tulsa, OK, USA: Harrison House, 1994), p81.

[7] Thayer's Greek Lexicon, taken from www.biblehub.com/greek/1343

[8] Kris Vallotton, 'Honor is one of the greatest attributes of nobility in the entire Bible. When the kingdom is present inside us, honorable behavior comes naturally to us. We give honor to all men not just because they deserve it, but also because we are honorable citizens of the King. – Supernatural Ways of Royalty book', Facebook post: 04/05/2014

[9] Ellicott's Commentary for English Readers, taken from www.biblehub.com/commentaries/nehemiah/8-10

[10] John McRay, 'Stench, Pain, and Misery', *Christianity Today*, Christian History, Issue 47, 1995, taken from www.christianitytoday.com/history

[11] Mother Teresa's prayer response to noted philosopher John Kavanaugh, 1975, Calcutta, India

[12] Efraim Goldstein, 'A Study on Biblical Concepts of Peace in the Old and New Testaments', 01/12/1997, taken from www.jewsforjesus.org/publications

[13] Edward Mote, *My Hope is Built on Nothing Less*, c.1834. Public domain.

[14] Oswald Chambers, *My Utmost for His Highest*, taken from www.utmost.org

Please note: all online content accessed and correct at time of writing (September 2017).

Inspiring
Women

Two ways to spend quality time with God